OUT OF THIS WORLD

POEMS FROM THE HAWKEYE STATE

OUT OF THIS WORLD

POEMS FROM THE HAWKEYE STATE

EDITED BY GARY GILDNER AND JUDITH GILDNER

THE IOWA STATE UNIVERSITY PRESS

AMES / 1975

Library of Congress Cataloging in Publication Data

Gildner, Gary, comp.
    Out of this world.

    1. American poetry—Iowa. 2. Iowa—Poetry. 3. Poetry of places—Iowa. I. Gildner, Judith, 1943–   joint comp. II. Title.
PS283.I8G54   811′.008   74–34153
ISBN 0–8138–1255–0

ACKNOWLEDGEMENTS

The editors and publisher thank the following publishers and individuals holding copyright for permission to reprint:

Mildred Kresensky Allen: "The Old Families" and "Windmill" from *Selected Poems* by Raymond Kresensky. By permission of Mildred Kresensky Allen.
Annals of Iowa: "Diary of an Iowa Farm Girl: Josephine Edith Brown, 1892–1901," ed. Vivian C. Hopkins. By permission of Judith Gildner. Pictograph, Wacochachi, text, Jack W. Musgrove and Mary R. Musgrove. By permission of Judith Gildner. "Elegy," James Hearst. By permission of Judith Gildner.
Richard Bissell: "Conversation in the Elite Café" from *7½ Cents*.
George Braziller, Inc.: "Nuisances" from *Whole Horse* by Kenneth Rosen; reprinted with the permission of the publisher. Copyright © 1973 by Kenneth Rosen. "Black Hawk in Hiding" and "He is Burning" from *Song in a Strange Land* by George Keithley; reprinted with the permission of the publisher. Copyright © 1974 by George Keithley.
Raymond Carver: "Iowa Summer 1967" from *Winter Insomnia*. Originally appeared in *Chelsea 22/23*.
Choice: "The Encumbrance," Dave Kelly. Originally appeared in *Choice 5*.
Josephine Clare: "the total length (for Valarie & Tom Raworth)," copyright © 1974 by Josephine Clare. From *deutschland & other places*, North Atlantic Books, Plainfield, Vermont, 1974. By permission of the author.
Crazy Horse: "How to Make Rhubarb Wine," Ted Kooser.
R. R. Cuscaden: "Cedar Rapids in the Morning." Originally appeared in *28 Poems*.
Stephen Dobyns: "High Society, Iowa City, Iowa" from *Concurring Beasts*, Stephen Dobyns, copyright © 1971 by Stephen Dobyns.
Doubleday & Company, Inc.: "The Eighty" from *We Have All Gone Away*, copyright © 1973 by Curtis Harnack. Reprinted by permission of Doubleday & Co., Inc.
Paul Engle: "For the Iowa Dead" from *Poems in Praise*. By permission of the author.
Dave Etter: "Old Dubuque" from *Go Read the River*. By permission of the author.
David Allan Evans: "The Cattle Ghosts." Originally appeared in *Poetry Northwest*.
Donald Finkel: "Target Practice" from *The Clothing's New Emperor and Other Poems*.
Gary Gildner: "Harry James & the Untuned Piano," Originally appeared in *Fiction International*.
The Greenfield Review: "From the Library Windows" and "Ice Fishing on the Mississippi," Ann Struthers.
Harper & Row, Publishers, Inc.: "Powwow" from *After Experience* by W. D. Snodgrass, copyright © 1962 by W. D. Snodgrass. Originally appeared in *The New Yorker*. Reprinted by permission of Harper & Row, Publishers, Inc.

iv

FOR GRETCHEN

CONTENTS

A NOTE

Here are one hundred one poems—all coming from Iowa—by sixty-eight writers. A few of the poems (Ann Darr's "Orders" or Lawrence Kramer's "The Largemouth Black Bass," for example) could easily reside in anthologies singing other midwestern states—or reside in any anthology for that matter; but we have them here because they did in fact come from Iowa.

The writers are not all native Iowans, however. That was not a prerequisite. The book's main business is the poems, and the different ways they look at Iowa. Some of these poems, incidentally, are in prose texts that we feel are lyrical; and one is a pictograph by an American Plains Indian, Wacochachi.

The idea for the book came one night when we found ourselves naming all the poems we could think of that might be called Iowa poems. After naming off a good number, it was inevitable we should begin thinking about collecting them. And why not? What better record of a region's cultural history than the poems it helps to cause? In looking around for others, we discovered a great many having to do with Iowa, not all of them fulfilled, to be sure. How many, finally, God only knows—the number we found on spring alone would fill, we daresay, half a dozen volumes, a most healthy sign.

In any case, we have surely missed some that deserve to be included. Also, we have had to leave out some we like very much, but whose concerns overlap the book's scheme or lie mainly elsewhere—Philip Dacey's "Looking at Models in the Sears Catalogue" and John Logan's "Saturday Afternoon at the Movies" are two of these we especially hated to give up.

We thank Anselm Hollo for allowing us to name the book after his own fine poem included here. And we thank the Iowa Arts Council for the support which helped to make this venture possible.

A final remark: one of the possible problems with books of a parochial bent is their grim, plodding sincerity. We hope we have collected a testament that speaks with character and dignity, is not without witness to those physical pleasures and pains that move us, and can laugh at itself, too.

GARY GILDNER
JUDITH GILDNER

September 15, 1974
Des Moines, Iowa

OUT OF THIS WORLD
POEMS FROM THE HAWKEYE STATE

IOWA SPRING VIEWED FROM A PLANE

I will not forget how black the earth is!
The grain elevator's sharp momentary 'O'
shifts, leans away and falls
across such fine geometry of fields.
Occasional roads slice through.
Dot of cow, of car,
no wayward fences here, all order here,
one white farmhouse and a barn and silo
where I can almost smell the corn
going sour, as if the earth were saying
(simply) to me, "Open like these fields."
There is a table, maybe, in that kitchen
where two persons sit who are in love,
perhaps touching, perhaps not, that tension
of distance being more exciting than touch;
between them a bowl with one yellow apple,
over which, the wind from the plane I'm in
makes a thin white curtain toss its shadow.

Jane Shore

4

ROMANCE

it is now known why the farmers
desert that fondling of their fields
why their wives give up the chickens
to the sly night that ferrets
the moon egg in the trough from between
the legs of the fence it is now
known why the children are hushed in
behind the lamps and the horses
excuse themselves into inconspicuous tufts
in the field's sleep because
it is embarrassing
this romance of empty space
that makes the open smell
of cowshit so untouchably near
that the white silo on the next farm
sweats with moonlight and accidentally
spills a slight stream of corn

Ed Roberson

SONG SPARROW

The year beginning with younger hope than ever!
—WALDEN

Oh it is spring again,
Maids! Maids! Maids!
hang up your teakettle-
ettle-ettle,

three long notes,
short ones,
trills—
hundreds

an april hour
—are you listening?
Maids! Maids! Maids!
grass is a bed

for bouncing,
the air is singing seed,
hang up your teakettle-
ettle-ettle,

tangle with me.
Maids! I am pacing
Milltown meadow
for your *eee eee eee.*

Raymond Roseliep

THE FARMER'S SEASON

Yeah, spring, I know spring, the vernal season,
the chores of birth bathed with lilac's perfume,
but the lily's gilt rubs off for the farmer's son
who keeps night-time vigils with mud and rain
and cold. Lord, what a way to inherit the earth,
aren't there other paths to life and the fullness
thereof? All this pain and blood and struggle
for a new start, all this sweat and moan to bring
forth, all this care, to clean nostrils and
let in air, to dry the body and warm the blood,
to teach wobbly legs to stand, the mouth to suck.
Here I am alone at midnight with the rain
for music, a bale of hay for my bed, a lantern
for light, and for company an old sow with
a basket of pigs in her belly ready to deliver.

James Hearst

DURING THE FIRST THREE MINUTES OF LIFE

The piglet
sucks

naps
wakes up

sniffs
the nipple next door

bites
his brother's ear

naps again
snores

wakes up
shivers

jumps straight up
twists an ankle

squeals
looks around for the sound

leaves home
gets lost

pees
on the run

stops on a window
frame of light

looks up
into the sun

Jim Heynen

TOURING THE HAWKEYE STATE

I saw the best parts of Iowa covered with New Jersey tea,
    partridge pea, rattlesnake master, and Culver's root,
    I saw Chief Keokuk's "X" in the county courthouse in Keokuk,
    home of John L. Lewis and Elsa Maxwell

I saw sweet William, wild rye, I saw the Iowa Watershed Divide
    running through the business district of Orient,
    I saw the outskirts of Adair and the locomotive wheel
    marking the spot where Jesse James derailed the Chicago,
    Rock Island and Pacific and knocked off engineer Rafferty
    and ran with the loot to Missouri

I saw gayfeather, blazing star, and butterfly weed,
    I saw where Henry Lott murdered Two Fingers on the banks
    of Bloody Run, where Dr. William S. Pitts, a dentist,
    wrote hymns, taught singing and practiced
    in Nashua in Chickasaw County,
    home of The Little Brown Church in the Vale,
    I saw Osage, home of Hamlin Garland

I saw the home of Iowa's only one-eyed governor, Bill Larrabee,
    and Clarinda, home of Glenn Miller,
    and Humboldt, home of Frank Gotch, who hammerlocked
    the Russian Lion Hackenschmidt for the world
    wrestling championship, and Grundy Center,
    home of Herbert Quick, author of *The Hawkeye,*
    The Invisible Woman, and others

I saw the braided rugs that Grant Wood's mother made
    from Grant's old jeans, where the *Bertrand* went down
    on her maiden voyage, taking boxes of Dr. Hostetter's
    Celebrated Stomach Bitters, and the Fairview Cemetery
    where Amelia Jenks Bloomer, of *The Lily,* lies buried,
    I saw her Turkish pantaloons

I saw the only Holstein museum in America
    and Mama Ormsby Burke's neck chain and milk stool

and the west branch of the Wapsinonoc and the modest
two-room cottage that sheltered young Herbert Hoover
and Peru where the first Delicious apple tree grew
and Newton, home of Emerson Hough, author of *Mississippi
Bubble*

I saw the summit of Floyd's Bluff and the lightning-
struck obelisk south of Sioux City
near Interstate 29, the final resting place
of the bones of Sergeant Charles Floyd
who died of a busted gut under Lewis and Clark,
their only loss on the whole trip,
I saw Oskaloosa where Frederic K. Logan
composed "Over the Hills" and "Missouri Waltz"

I saw the Walnut, Turkey, Pony, Plum, and Honey creeks,
the Polecat River, Spirit Lake, the park where John Brown
drilled for Harper's Ferry, Eisenhower's Mamie's
home in Boone, the home of John "Duke" Wayne, née Marion M.
Morrison, in Winterset, Billy Sunday's mother's grave
a peg from Story County's Sewage Plant,
where Billy saw the light, where he came back
to gather souls, in Garner, after shagging flies in center
for the Chicago White Stockings

I saw ½ mile west of Orient where Henry Agard Wallace,
experimentalist and Republican, Democrat and Progressive,
breeder of chickens, strawberries, and hybrid corn
and Iowa's only U.S. Vice President was born,
on a nine-acre tract of virgin Iowa prairie
in West of Orient I saw pink and white beardtongue

I saw where Jenny Lind and Tom Thumb appeared
in Stone City, where Cyphert Talley, a Baptist preacher,
was killed in the Talley or Skunk River War
in Sigourney, where the Sac-Fox council
started the Black Hawk War in Toolesboro,
where Chief Wapello and his friend General Street
are buried in the same plot along the C. B. & Q.
right-of-way in Agency

I saw the trails worn in the sod by trekking Mormons,
the Corning farm of Howard Townsend, historic communist,
blue-eyed grass and Jerusalem artichoke,
war clubs, knives, scrapers, grinders, and threshers,
hickory, basswood, hackberry, wahoo, and burr,
a Victorian parlor, a low-growing yew,
a rare folding bathtub, a belfry stocked with birds

Gary Gildner

ORDERS

After I ran away from home and came back again,
my Papa said, Go if you must but mind three things:
stay away from water, stay off of boats, and don't
go up in an aeroplane.   So first I learned to swim,
then I learned to sail,   and then I learned to fly.

Ann Darr

IOWA: TORNADO WEATHER

The mare went crazy last July,
the cows all flattened milking pails and fell
asleep—the barn fell down on pa.
Meanwhile the tractor wouldn't quit, bounced up
and ran along the Dawkins' fence toward town.
Granny took a lover, the hired man's hair
turned purple, blew away—
The pancakes ma made rolled into the yard,

sliced the legs off twenty chickens,
are still rolling.
            And, let me see,
instead of growing in the fields,
the corn came through the bathroom floor
and tasseled, pigs walked in and watched,
a goose climbed onto sissie's head and
wouldn't leave—frogs appeared, a cat
turned inside out, became a nest of wasps
and several spiders . . . last July
when it was hot and dry and golly
it was something else.

                                Dennis Trudell

TARGET PRACTICE

On the first day good enough father and son
Went out with the new gun
And rode for miles in Iowa.

No. That spring, city-bred and new to sun,
We went out in the car in Iowa
And parked at last between
Two farms and walked, through mud, to the place.

Neither is right, the fiction
Or the fact. It is as if
What happened were good enough, as if the place,
If I described it, might produce
Shoots between the wagon-ruts,
As the spring works, yearly, miracles in Iowa.
No poem grows anything.
The hands of words are tender,
False to work, as you and I were false, in Iowa,
To mud and gun, were neither

Farmer's son nor father,
Whose ancient secrets back away from words
Like huge and hungry birds
That have no use for song.

A poem is the least kind of honesty. Words
Have their sense and semblance.
When I saw, over the place,
The huge bird angling, I said, It's a hawk,
It's a hawk, and you could
Shoot then, at something,
Even if it was a crow we saw, and not a hawk
At all.

But a poem is the least
kind of honesty. It's to subsist
In woods for weeks on weeds to tell your friends
How you and nature are like
That. One must, to speak
Directly, have, at first, something to say to friends,
To sons. That spring in Iowa
We shot skyward at the hawk,
The crow, in a copse between two farms. We hit
Nothing, I think, though three
Times the big bird suddenly,
For a silent moment, fell, as if we'd really hit
Him, then changed direction
And wheeled off, screaming.

We did not hit him, I think, and I don't know
If it was a hawk or a crow
We didn't hit that day,
Between two populated farms, and I don't know
Where the bullets finally
Went, or if they killed
Some farmer, maybe, or his son, someone who knew
Hunting, mud, knew guns, who
Spoke little, having little

To say, could tell a hawk from a crow, and knew
His father, maybe, the way you
Don't know me, or I know you.

Donald Finkel

THE MARAUDER

When they shot the bear out of his tree,
North, on Monday, in Cedar County,
It occurred to us the bear knew, too,
Something was not enough—a stirring,
A yearning for sweetness buried deep
In the shrunk gut, portentous forage.
We knew and he knew: it was something
Not to perish of capture, sloven
And soft from caramel corn, smarting
With mange under the fur, with cinders
Lodged in the cracked pads. Something—at least
Not a cage—but not truly enough.
When they shot the bear out of his tree,
A single shot, and the limber trunk
Yawed with the target, sprang back, sang out
As green wood does in the springtime, stopped—
When the bear chose to drop, swam the air
Littered by yellow buds, pulled with him
The slim top twigs to the populous
Field—the tree bled; the earth at its roots
Shook and worms far under felt: waking.
For them, too, not enough, but something.

Robley Wilson, Jr.

THE SPIDER

This afternoon I swept up her body
And the flaccid egg-sac, grey with cellar dust.
This time I knew she was dead. A day or two ago,
Touched by the broom, she clutched the egg-sac convulsively
With all her long legs, even though it was empty then,
Or all the young were dead. And, though they make me uneasy,
If only because they are so big, and I don't really want the cellar
    thickly inhabited
With furry spiders, I grieved for this one.

I'd watched her a long time with that egg-sac
When it was still white and globular, adhering to her abdomen,
And she was still free to move, though little inclined.
She had travelled a long way with it, considering its size
And the possible ratio of its weight to hers—in the heat, too—
(Even the cellar is warm in an Iowa summer.)
I suppose she moved more freely when I turned out the lights.

Where did her kind live before my kind dug cellars here, I wonder,
And on what?   I never saw her leading a silk line
Or watching one of the countless snares I have dislodged when they
    caught my face in the dark.
She stood still on the wall, as long as my thumb, her fur as fine
    as velvet,
And I think it was she who picked bare
All those fragments of beetle carapace
I have swept up once a week for so long,
Absorbing their acrid smell with every breath.
(It is in my bones now. I shall never be rid of it.)

And I think she was our hostess the evening the sirens
Screamed above the wind, sending us to the cellar with the carved
    mirror,
My four best flutes and a pitcher of martinis.
The beetle smell was strong that night. We drank it.

We could not see her but we knew she was near,

Extending a sort of toleration, if not a welcome,
Whether or not she recognized the fact
That the unpredictable, absolute, illogical forces of destruction
Were now themselves in jeopardy.

Today I dropped her body into the trash can
Wondering what had become of the progeny she lived and died for,
I looked and looked but I could see them nowhere.

Myra Mayo

TAKE-OFF

(From a pond in Iowa)

The gangling,
gathering-for
flight, leg-
catapulted,
clapper-lifted,
clapper-
wafted,
wing-span-wide
white heron,
one-bird cloud,
gets a leg
up on the
horizon.

Ernest Kroll

FIELD

The hogs' little houses standing in the rain
the clear-eyed pig knee-deep in gulley water

Mark Doty

WINDMILL

A bald eagle
Hangs over the barn yard
Beating his wings spasmodically
And screaming,
Fighting the wind.
When the tank is filled
I forget him.

Raymond Kresensky

THE LARGEMOUTH BLACK BASS

Bass, only you were sacred
when I was little
fishing the small pond where everything grew
to full size, so balanced
you kept it, reaping
the weak, the unnecessary.
I prayed for you with the ugliest things
I could carve,
small, helpless, noisy creatures.
I made their heads bleed;
I danced and teased

them through your hideout
(What was there for you to hide from?)
in the one action you can't resist,
terror in the unnatural,
fish that wallow on the surface, wooden,
with propellers,
rubber skirts, spinners polished
to absolute reflexion.
I loved your Godlike economy
of movement—your lazy, thin,
broad tail content
to hold you in merest suspension—
and your boney, plated jaws opened,
the largest part of you.
You were more me
than I could ever be:
your indolent meanness;
I saw you kill
for the hell of it, eat,
regurgitate to eat again.
Your suspicious indifference I took
for my intelligence.
When you let me set
my treble hooks in you,
usually in the dense indigo moments
before electrical storms,
you walked, a frenzy, on the water
shook your head no, no, no
snapped the lure back at eye level.
If I landed you,
I let you go back unharmed.
Call it weakness or preservation
of balance.
Call it arrogance:
I walked home in the flooding, charged, eroding earth
certain of the safe passage.

Lawrence Kramer

ICE FISHING ON THE MISSISSIPPI

Inside the fish house
black, black out of the wind
the augered elipse
in the twelve-inch ice glows,
light comes from the river, blue,
cold, and fish fin slow,
ignoring the bait,
suspended in liquid light
safe from leaping summer
and strange meat.
Here in the slick dark
I slip
into the eye of the fish,
down, down into the deeper pools
of the water, move into the underground river
far below the crust
which flows through the unknown country.

Ann Struthers

MISSISSIPPI

oh jesus christ what a fine
river   I love you   and
why not, remember exactly
the first time I saw you

Clinton,   the old bridge
unsafe my mother said   we were
on the way to Cedar Rapids
and there you were, oh
bigger than any airport   or
how about that spring time in

Davenport when it was flooding
or that other time in Davenport
Jane and I were down by the river
July 4, 1964 at noon and just then
all the bells in town rang
                    or
Eagle Point Park in Dubuque, we
stopped to use up film and saw
the antique car show and you
spread below just like the map
said, only bigger   prettier

and standing and looking down
for catfish holes downstream
of islands, walleye spots
in the millrace below the dam
oh you big fine river I want
to spend the rest of my life fishing

and I don't care what they say
about you, erosion, pollution
anything   I wouldn't even care
if the bridge gave way   I'd float
to New Orleans, I'd be part of you
all the bells would ring

Phillip Hey

HOUSES: OUT

Isolated. Located off
from the house, you can
believe that. A swarm

of interested flies loitering
there, multiplying. A sure
nest of wasps beneath the roof

no one could resist whacking
with brooms and ball bats.
Be out there meal time, no one

would come to fetch you in.
Drop a quarter, gone forever.
The place to smoke illegal

cigarettes, sit too long
to dodge chores, read those
Sears and Wards catalogs cover

to cover. Wonder, casually,
if it might not have been
a nickel you dropped.

Victoria McCabe

GENUINE POEM, FOUND ON A BLACKBOARD
IN A BOWLING ALLEY IN STORY CITY, IOWA

If you strike
when head pin
is red pin,
one free game
to each line.
Notify desk
before you throw
if head pin
is red

Ted Kooser

IOWA SUMMER 1967

The paperboy shakes me awake. "I have been dreaming you'd come,"
I tell him, rising from the bed. He is accompanied
By a giant Negro from the university who seems
Itching to get his hands on me. I stall for time.
Sweat runs off our faces; we stand waiting.
I do not offer them chairs and no one speaks.

It is only later, after they have gone,
I realize they have delivered a letter from my wife.
"What are you doing there?" my wife asks. "Are you drinking?"
I study the post mark for hours until it, too, begins to fade.
Someday, I hope to forget all this.

Raymond Carver

TWO RENEWAL POEMS

1 *The Line*

What weather is this?
My body is heavy, real; it walks
Out of the house, into the wind.
My small son watches from the window;
I wave and walk away.
A bluejay stalls
Above a spruce. My
Forehead touches the cold glass.
My father waves
And walks away.

2 *The Circle*

Driving across Iowa
in the corn-green light, you
sometimes come across

between the road and pasture
a knee-high gush of water
from a deep artesian well
rising and tumbling into itself
in the raw sun, cold and sweet.

You stand at the center of summer,
your life rising and falling.

Take a tin can from the fencepost.
Drink.

David Young

OUR FARM/OUR FAMILY

Land there in Iowa lay so flat
we never dared run naked through the fields
and only joked of swimming nude
in the creek so close to the railroad.
Now and then we did pee in the clover
but only on dark nights when the neighbors
were inside with their four-cornered eyes.

All roads there were straight,
barns rode the horizon like ships,
the sun was hours in setting,
and on the heaviest summer nights
a laugh could be heard for a mile.
We learned to be cautious as that albino fox
the whole township hunted for years.

So we were never exposed
except to ourselves on Saturday nights
when, just after eight, our family of five

conspired in the dim-lit kitchen,
stark-naked around the galvanized tub.
We laughed and pinched and took turns
scrubbing and using the same water.

Sunday morning the wide church pews
were the final test. We passed: Father,
Brother, and I in our black suits and starched collars;
Mother, tightened in her corset, black hat and veil;
Sister, too fully developed, draped in her loose
brassiere and the dress that kept everything private.
We liked things this way: the inside, the out.

Jim Heynen

IN MY FATHER'S FIELD

We walked out aways to check
the crops: soybeans this time
of year could use more rain,
he explained. He pulled horseweeds
from the rows, cursed the meddling
morning glories. The rat terrier
ran, crazy, for rabbits, gophers.
The goodness of Dad's 40-acre
air! I turned and held a clod
of earth, stuffed it in my mouth.
Tasted expensive. Like caviar
and certain kinds of cheese:
was it *bad* or supposed to taste
like that? The land swelled
upon my tongue, gritted
among my teeth. Dad asked
was I hungry. What could I say,
my mouth full of his heritage?

We walked on back to the house,
ate roast pig and fresh boiled greens.

Victoria McCabe

THE IOWA PLETHORA TREE

for Marvin Bell & Mark Strand

I

If there is but one tree,
and that one
at great distance,
its importance
is found in perspective,
the relationship of eye to distance,
married to height.

II

In an evening between seasons
there is a swimmer wind
that moves slowly for the tree:
have we passed it?
Is it still ahead?—
wind without voice.

III

This is the hill that anywhere
else is prairie dog plot,
the sun a star on mound-peak.
This is eye-path we head onto
for pleasure, the pathetic
when we need composure and return
without need to find ourselves—
domesticated like good wood.

IV
Nevermind if this one living thing
lifts into air with your movement.
Everything here is fine,
plumed or branched.
A background of snow is all
one needs to lift the poor arms
of the lone pine of the plains.

V
I am one who has lived near water—
In the sleeping sea wind
of the Pacific,
in the exactness of the east
where the Atlantic spits upon a beach.
A different kettle of fish here—
a single tree, the big freeze
that sends the ice-sky
down your spine in winter.
Nevermind, you who know the coasts,
the cold will find a home—
forget the balance of the tides.

VI
We grind ourselves to dirt
we grind ourselves
we grind
we
who grind ourselves to dirt

VII
Keep your distance, fingers of air,
the great tree bears us,
fruit.

Daniel Halpern

WHAT THE BRIDE SAW

The hottest afternoon in August,
three gilts nosed under the fence,
rooted up the new garden until
the man raged out of the house,
swearing, running.

For fifty minutes he chased to get
them in. One snorted its pure
defiance, would not be guided
to the hoglot, wore the man
to a humid frazzle. He'd had
all he would take; found a two-by-four
near the shed. Swung it, for practice,
in mid-air.

He would never talk, later, of how
he clubbed the pig in a corner, chopping
at its hide until it collapsed, grunting
and snorting, the bright blood splotching
up the fence they'd painted "Barnyard
White" the week before. He couldn't
stop chopping.

No one now would believe it, she often
thought, after the years of his deep
silence, after seeing him walk away
from a fight or two. But she knew
the passion in him, and worked to keep
on his good side.

Victoria McCabe

from DIARY OF AN IOWA FARM GIRL

Jan. 4, 1897

I cried tonight. We were downstairs after supper sitting around
the table and John was popping corn. We were teasing Louis and
pretty soon he gave me a cuff beside the head and I came upstairs
and cried and cried all to myself. Big brute he is anyway. Emma
came up pretty soon and wanted to know what was the matter. I had
been crying. Then Mama came up and talked to me. She is so good
and told me I knew what Louis was and mustn't cry about him. She
says she prays for him every day of her life, but says she don't know
what makes him be so gruff. It did me good to cry, and I told Mama
it is so hard to be good, and I can't help from saying and thinking
the mean things. She says Pa is so cranky it makes her that way too,
but she is trying to be gentle, poor dear Mamma. I didn't know she
had to try to be good. I thought the Christian life would get easier
after you lived in it a long time.

Josephine Edith Brown

WHAT SHE TOLD THE SHERIFF

Hot nights out in the cornshocks,
    Snakelike they'd go
Bashing about in pickup trucks,
    Headlights on low,
Staking out soft beds in Hell,
    Giggling. Till morning,
Safe on my windowsill,
    I'd do the darning,
Three-way lamp all the way up,
    Hymns turned on louder,
Knees tight locked, china cup
    Of headache powder

Running over. I'd kiss Christ
   (My own right arm)
Or read till, my eyes crossed,
   Red words would squirm.
I'd pray: Change places, Lord,
   Stroke by stroke the corn
Watched You nailed back on Your board
   Sure as You're born.
Lend me the power to damn
   Those lipsticked, caving
Doors to man's battering-ram.
   What one's worth saving?—
No sign. Only the moon's gleam,
   Monotonous tick talk
From the wall clock, shine of ice cream
   Bowls from the dish rack,
Four years locked in a frame
   Instead of marriage:
The sheepskin bearing my name
   Like some miscarriage.
Paul said, *Our days in earth*
   Are as a shadow . . .
Father no doubt slept with
   His plump grass-widow
While Mother courted sleep,
   As ever ailing,
Spending life's ocean trip
   Hugged to the railing.
Next noon, out choosing ears
   For the lunch pot,
I'd come on sin's arrears
   Still body-hot:
There in the scrambled dirt
   The telltale pressings
Of buttocks, a torn-off shirt,
   Love's smelly passings.
Father, how could Your Hand
   Deign to forgive?

Smite them! Don't understand,
    Don't just let live!
I'd weep, the sun's broadsword
    Carving my bonnet,
For this blood-handed world
    And all here on it.
Then one noon, my Maker's ways
    Laid themselves bare.
Scabs fell down from my eyes,
    All stood forth clear:
Worms, worms in leaf and ear,
    Kernel and tassel,
Gnawing the Wurlitzer
    In Burger Castle!
Hell peered through surgeon's slits,
    Burst out of faucets—
Babies chopped off at the root,
    Crushed flat in corsets!
My heart caught fire in me,
    Fire hard to cover—
How endlessly time marks time
    When God's your lover—
And it was all I could do
    Till my right hour
To hold a lid over my glow,
    Sifting cake flour.
Midnight. Led by my sword,
    Ripe for reborning,
I strode in where Dad snored,
    Mother lay turning:
Two old and swollen sheep
    Stretched out for slaughter,
Teeth set adrift to keep
    In mineral water,
They were like chopping wood.
    Drunk, uncomplaining,
And wondering Dad stood
    A long while draining.

Mother half raised her, coughed,
 Said—for once painless—
Girl, wipe that cleaver off,
 That one's not stainless.
Next, blazing kerosene
 Wiped the brown oily
Head-shaped time-honored stain
 From Dad's chair doily.
Along the henhouse path,
 Dry faggots crackled.
At each step I shook earth with
 The bantam cackled.
Saint Michael goaded me,
 Grass fire his halo,
Render unto Your Father on high
 Your father's silo!
Wrath roared in my right hand,
 How soon it catched
Where, like deceivers' tents,
 Hay sat pitched.
Creatures of hoof and horn,
 Sheol's lumps of tallow,
Struck at walls of their barn
 That soon grew hollow.
Far as earth led the eye,
 Smoke bloomed, burnt stubble
Crawled legless. It was I
 Cast down the Devil.
Why did you handcuff me?
 Let go! By morning
All Iowa could be
 One high bush, burning.

         X. J. Kennedy

LITTLE BULL

The . . . poor . . . little . . . bull
behind the gate calls to
cows knee deep in clover,
the wind smells of cows in clover,
the sun stains his back with
sweat where flies gather,
he bangs the gate, barbed wire
sinks its teeth into his hide
and he bleeds, down in the dust
he kneels and bawls, red-eyed,
furious, his groin aches and swells,
the steel sings in its muscle,
he's just a little black bull
butting his horns against the
damnedest bull-tight gate
you ever saw.

James Hearst

THE WHEEL OF SUMMER

The dark land rose in the luminous arch of sky.
The bald sun softly grew. Down by the barn
My father and we three sons watched how it fell
Through hazes of sour dust by the old pig pens.
"They got away from us," my father said.
He didn't need to say it. The great sun god
Bowed to the grassy sea by the western hills,
Darkened to blood, rolled in the tasseled corn
And flamed our blinking eyeballs. "Yup," we said,
And turned in the dirty twilight to our thoughts.

Those silken shoats with jiggling nuts
Went squealing under their mothers' tits

Two months too long, until they ran
Smelling each other around the pens
And snuffled into a herd of lusts.
Ourselves but fifteen, fourteen, twelve,
We knew that wrestling those young boars
And bearing them, sterile, up from the knives
With bristling feet and foaming mouths
Could bend our steel and twist our smiles.

We ambled, loose in overalls, up by the house.
We doused our barny hands in sun-warmed waters,
Waited for supper, glanced at the girls, then ate.
We counted a few odd stars and the evening star
Over the glut of summer. Later, upstairs,
We stripped and gathered a pillow into our arms,
Rolled in the humid nightfall once or twice,
Muttered a thing or two, then fell asleep.

The women swept the kitchen,
Carried the washing waters,
Scrubbing towels and basins.
We slept. They quietly chatted,
Loosened their hair and spread it
In puffs for summer dreaming.

Out of those dreaming coves
The dawn broke, suddenly,
And rolled the milk-dust haze
Up Bekkan's Ridge. We yawned,
Straightened the slack in our mouths,
Tightened our muscles a notch,
Wrinkled our groins like a gourd,
And marched on out to the barn.

Then father called, "Let's drive them in."
We harried pigs toward the dusty barn,
Kicked the shoats and rammed the door
And banged the bar in its wooden home.
Coarse as our job, we whaled them all

Till some walked, upright, on the gates
And flowed together. "Wet them down!"
In the stock-tank our buckets swam,
Slipped and swished and, bellying up,
Went shivering over the slithering pens.
Our badgered strength was out of mind
In summer madness: a sty of sounds.

Our father, priest and teacher, led us on.
We stood in the sire's circle while he talked,
Whipped out his knife and whetted it on stone.
He flipped some acrid lysol from his jug
To test it out, then touched the slicing blade
Gingerly over his thumb. All set to go.
"Boys, let's bring them on." We'd bring them on.

> We eyed the mob,
> Curious, queasy.
> Grey dust flowered
> Under the rafters.
> Breathy and muddy,
> They surged together
> In sour odors.

The three of us dove down the herd.
I grabbed one, dared not let him go.
Some boyish pride threw out my arms
To catch the unsuspecting world.
They clamped like iron. Crushing him,
I locked him to my chest and bore
Him, staggering, to the trough. Hair,
Plastered with dust, bristled my arms.
"Hup, flip him now!" Damned if I didn't,
But square on his feet. Off he ran,

His bony tail stretched outward from my hands,
He charged the herd. I hauled him down again,
And up from the pigsty floor we two arose,

Loudly embracing. And for what purposes?
"Hang on this time!" You think I would've lost him?
I knew when we were working, not at games,
When to be gentle, when to play it rough;
One cannot breed ten thousand animals
Into this world and woo them for the axe
Without a curse and prayer to help him through.

     I got him upside down in the trough
     And hung on his heels. I stomped his chest.
     My brother locked his squealing snout.
     With lysol, tender flesh was doused;
     That knife dipped in the slickest stroke
     I ever saw this side of hell,
     And murderous music, like a crime,
     Gurgled that milk-blue blooded dream.

Snip went the cords; the mindless body doubled.
Flick went the blade again; the shades of change
Rolled down the dust beyond the feeding troughs,
A tough abstraction. Dropping the crippled pig,
We rolled him out and ran him down the alley.
He walked so gingerly he seemed to dance
With quivering hooves upon the ragged straw
Along the barn. The solemn way he went,
He must have dumbly felt some ancient law
Driving him out of nature's benediction.

        Infected with truth,
        We hung in dust
        Drenched to our skins,
        Bleached to our bones.
        He sat in the straw
        Mute as a rock,
        Crudely undone.
        Ranker than swine,
        Coarse to our nails
        We swung to our job.

Then we went all the way
To common terms with loss.

Having run down our guilt and pain,
We lobbed the curses from our mouths.

We trapped them all. We never bore so much
Next to our hearts. We caught them with our feet,
Caged them for death and shrilled them back to life
To trot, untroubled, fattening for your grace.
So we prepared your table. The awful world
Seemed natural as breathing. Brazen with swine,
We hounded the living daylights out of the earth.
Nature we rolled, denatured, in the straw
Where loss waits in the alleys like a snake,
Coiled and ready, although it cannot strike.
The last lay down exhausted, wouldn't run.
We could have lain down with him. Had he fought
We might have, in our weakness, let him go.
At last, we spun the gates and turned them out
Under the burroak trees by the young alfalfa.
The barrows wandered through the blooming grasses.
We poured some water for their healing mudbaths.
We filled their troughs with generous sour mashes.
Burying snouts, they snuffled in rows of pigs' eyes,
And we, stinking high heaven, turned and trotted
Slowly along the woodpaths into the valley.

How shall I praise the valley waters,
The crystal springs so sweetly aching
Over our bruised, our lusty bodies?

We slid in water like sluggish wishes
And lay on sandbanks, mute and weary.
The water idled over our heartbeats.

We blew cool water out of our noses
With the clotted curses and grey mucus
And rose in our summer limbs for drying.

From sparkling stones we walked; then, dressing
In cleanest clothes on the polished gravels,
We stretched ourselves on yielding grasses,

While healing evening came.
We felt another dream
Rise in our flesh and feed
The mouth of mysteries;
It flickered in our minds
And quivered in our thighs.
Sweeping across our limbs,
It loosed our fumbling tongues
Until, at last, we talked
About the neighbor girls
And joked among ourselves.

We rose from the banks. For the evening star
Our casual wishes and shadowy groves
Welled with a tougher grace. To the barn
We rocked with the great maternal cows
And milked them down with our gentlest hands.

Next morning took us like an old surprise.
Fallen, with old corruption in our arms,
We praised the animal urgencies of love,
Our long obedience. The mind of man,
Boyishly wandering out of the eye of God,
Seemed natural to our wills. Our bruised bones
Took on this sweet admission. Proud in the sun,
Calloused and cocked, wicked and wise and young,
We ran, three golden idols, back to chores,
Shouldered the wheel of summer, and journeyed on.

Joseph Langland

NIGHT ON CLINTON

The bar is closed and I come
to myself outside the door,
drunk and shivering. The talking
champions, the bedroom
killers, the barroom Catholics
have all drifted away and I
am standing in a yellowish
wound of light. Above the blot
my breathing makes on the glass,
I look down the darkened bar
where the bottles are out of breath,
the stale tumblers bunched, and white
glistening webs in the pitchers
dry up and shrivel.
The plastic stools turn
in the hot light that bubbles
from the big Sea Bird, silent now,
and a shape vaguely human
moves with a rag and a limp
among the tables
piled high with surrendered chairs.
Nailed on the back wall, a great
Canadian elk fixes me
with his glazed liquid eyes and
the last lights go out. What I see
is important now, but I see
only the dim half-moon
of my own face in the black
mirror of space, and I lay
my cheek against the cold glass.
Snow is beginning to fall,
huge wet flakes that burst from
the darkness like parachutes
and plunge past the streaming light
and melt into the street.
Freeze, die, says the veteran wind

from the north but he goes on
with his work, the night and the snow,
and was not speaking to me.

Robert Mezey

MORGAN'S CANES

Morgan had a limp. When he was twenty-nine
he caught his right foot in a trap his brother set
for bear, and because of this he took to making canes.
When he bought new sows and plowed the pig-yard wider
than it was before, he saved what larger roots
the shoats might waste themselves upon or hurt their snouts.
They made for better walking, or a sure support
for conversation when the talk was interrupted
by a sudden waft from overalls, or he felt
the time had come for hawking spit and pounding it
to punctuate the graveness of a point. They were
always gnarled and bronzed, the canes I mean, like pine
you sometimes see in the woods, where bark has split high
in the tree so evening light reflects on it like sun
on a polished shield or burnished amber, and made from wrist-sized
wood, the kind old-timers used to bend their backs
to when the plows got stuck. He'd cure them for a year,
then close the grain with an old sow's bone, just like a big
league player with his favorite bat. "Nothin' like
a sow for sealin' right, the way the tourists shut
car windows when they pass my place!" he'd shout, near twelve
o'clock at Hamm's each Friday night, standing at
the bar and striking the cane against the darker wood,
just to demonstrate the point as fact, or just
in case some younger buck, knowing it was Morgan
and the smell that made him rich now ripe enough
to air his pride, might care to hold his nose and laugh.

John Judson

NUISANCES OF WINTER

for B.R.D.

And I, despite the bitterness of the cold,
the snow, its falling on the crawling traffic's
headlights, the lit and drafty passages, fumes
of exhaust, and breath, and of stores, traffic-
lights, life red, yellow, green, in this little
city, a snatch of bricks, the sky black, where
stars appear if you peer up for them, light like snow,
in dead pursuit, a certain kind of friend, my inferior,
hating me nervously, busy, seeking distance—O,
friend, I've followed all my life, to beg forgiveness!
Selecting from identical doors, old restaurants,
taverns, KENNY'S in Iowa City six years later,
without the old man, or Irene, and yet the jukebox,
and yet the same shadows and light, the dangerous
strangers at the bar, in booths, was perfectly
barechested, even hairless. That friend, vanished
in the yellow air and blackness, a wraith forgot,
as I pressed past Anna, the barmaid, and patrons
pivoting on their stools grew glowing, friendly: man
with long brown hair, skin covered chest, full beard,
muscling into the rest room marked MEN. I pissed,
seeking to miss the trouser legs of trousers hung
from hooks on ceiling pipes, yet splashed and turned
their bottoms wet and dark and black. My piss
was running down a drain. I switched, at last,
to a urinal proper, yet still saw trouser legs
obstructing me and catching my splashes. I put on
a starched white shirt, its short sleeves neatly
slashed, my triceps and biceps dramatic, its linen
body belling about my torso, sail on a strong mast,
until tucked in my pants. I went back. "Willy,
I'm surprised at you," I heard Anna say. Way
in the deep end of the bar I stood. I shone
with my new light. "Be not surprised. Every
intricacy, delight, is plant and seed. Today is

mother of all days, all days the mother of today."
Then I saw them, snowflakes, plying, multiplied
by thousands, men puffing cigarettes, drinking beer,
altering motes and lakes of light, waiting all night
for links to melt, freeze, or get shoveled. Snow!
O night serene! Outside light traffic passes, prowls.

Kenneth Rosen

THE MISSISSIPPI BETWEEN

I lie watching seeds of light spill from the pomegranate
heart of town across the river,
my hand within reach of a wild lily.

Raymond Roseliep

JOHANN GAERTNER (1793-1887)

In the blue winter of 1812
Johann Gaertner, a bag of bones,
followed Napoleon home.
He was cold; Napoleon,
riding ahead under a bear
wrap, fumed at the lice
in his hair.   —From Moscow
to Borodino, from Borodino
to the Baltic Sea, Napoleon
fumed and slapped, and glared hard
at the gray shapes
pushing at his face.

And maybe ate a piece of fruit
he did not taste. If he
cried, we do not know it.
But Johann Gaertner, 19,
a draftee, a bag of bones,
blew on his fingers
and bit them, and kicked at his toes.
And chewed and chewed
a piece of pony gristle.
And once, trying to whistle
an old dog into his coat,
swallowed a tooth.
God save Johann!, Johann
Gaertner, 19, cried,
moving his two blue feet
through bloody holes his eyes
kept staring and staring at . . .
And in the midst of all this
one night God appeared, hoary and fat,
and yelled at him in Russian,
Kooshat! Kooshat!—
and Johann closed his eyes
waiting for one of his sharp white bones
to pierce his heart.
When none did, he dragged them
past the mirror Napoleon
gazed and gazed at his rasp-
berry-colored chin in . . .
and past windy St. Helena
where his former leader was already lost
among the washed-up herring.
And Johann kept going,
picking up crumbs like a sparrow!—
no longer hearing that tooth
grinding against his ribs,
but starting to feel the sun
on the back of his neck
for a change, and loving the itch

and salty wash of sweat
everywhere on his chest.
             And one day
holding up a jug of cool switchel,
he had swig upon swig upon swig
and felt his whole blessed mouth
turn ginger—
and he whispered a song
that came out *Ah, Johann* . . .
        Thus,
having stopped, he stepped back
and took in his fields of hay,
his acres and acres of feed,
and his six black bulls
bulging against the sky.
And sitting down he ate
the giant mounds of sweet
red cabbage his ample wife
set before him,
and the pickled corn,
and the mashed potatoes dripping
galaxies of gizzards, hearts,
and juicy bits of wing,
and yet another slice
of her salt-rising bread
spread with his own
bee-sweetened butter.
(Often Johann stretched out big
in the clover, listening to his bees,
churn, churn, they said, *churn* . . .)
And praising God while licking his fingers
he allowed for a wedge of her
sour cream raisin pie,
and a mug of steaming
coffee out on the porch,
where he liked to stick his stockinged feet
among the fireflies,
and feel the slow closing

of his eyes . . .
          And all of this
(including the hickory nut cake,
rhubarb wine, and the fine old fat-
bellied kitchen stove)
happened for many years
in little Festina, Iowa,—
where Anton Dvorak came to drink
local Bohemian beer
and hear the Turkey River;
and where rosy Johann Gaertner
dug down deep in the rich black dirt
to make his own hole
and one for his wife as well.

Gary Gildner

HOW TO MAKE RHUBARB WINE

Go to the patch some afternoon
in early summer, fuzzy with beer
and sunlight, and pick a sack
of rhubarb (red or green will do)
and God knows watch for rattlesnakes
or better, listen: they make a sound
like an old lawnmower rolled downhill.
Wear a hat. A straw hat's best
for the heat but lets the gnats in.
Bunch up the stalks and chop the leaves off
with a buck-knife and be careful.
You need ten pounds; a grocery bag
packed full will do it. Then go home
and sit barefooted in the shade
behind the house with a can of beer.
Spread out the rhubarb in the grass

and wash it with cold water
from the garden hose, washing
your feet as well. Then take a nap.
That evening, dice the rhubarb up
and put it in a crock. Then pour
eight quarts of boiling water in,
cover it up with a checkered cloth
to keep the fruit flies out of it,
and let it stand five days or so.
Take time each day to think of it.

When the time is up, dip out the pulp
with your hands for strainers; leave the juice.
Stir in five pounds of sugar
and an envelope of Red Star yeast.
Ferment ten days, under the cloth,
sniffing of it from time to time,
then siphon it off, swallowing some,
and bottle it. Sit back and watch
the liquid clear to honey-yellow,
bottled and ready for the years,
and smile. You've done it awfully well.

Ted Kooser

THE FARM JOURNAL SILVER JUBILEE
COUNTRY COOKBOOK

Illustrations and diction! O take
me back to the cornfields and acre-
size gardens, Sunday suppers and home
canning. A whole fat section on Pies:
Tawny Pumpkin, Rosy Crab Apple, and Burgundy
Berry; Crinkly Meringue and Flaky Basic
Crusts (picture them: tenderly brown,

delicate and cooling). Turn to page two-
forty-nine: Rummage Pickle Relish
chock full of head cabbage and cucumber.
There's Braised Rabbit and Roast Fresh
Ham; Boys' Breakfast Sandwiches for Dad's
tractor helpers, and Garden Row Soup,
substantial, a treat! Country butter
and Whole Wheat Waffles oh warm from the stove
served at dawn's first crackle: Pull up
a chair. Say grace. Move out of town.

Victoria McCabe

CORN SALAD

18 large ears of corn cut from the cob
7 green peppers chopped fine
7 large onions chopped fine
1 large cabbage chopped fine
3 c sugar
½ c salt
2 qts vinegar
1½ tbsp celery seed
2 tbsp dry mustard
2 tbsp flour
Wet mustard and flour and mix all together.
Boil for one and a half hours. Seal in hot jars.

Mrs. Harry (Bertha) Kirkendall

COME NEAR THE WESTERN EDGE, I TRY A LAST MYTH FOR THE CHILDHOOD OF MY SONS

"The giant is eating the mountain,"
I tell my children while eating
cereal with them.
                    A gray moustache
is working slowly down the last green
slope before ours. It is a very large
                    mountain
and mostly granite. It is very hard. It
                    is
much harder than limestone, which was
formed from small shellfish under the sea
                    in Iowa.
    "Our old home under ocean?"
                    "Yes, once upon a time
an ocean ate little Iowa."
                    "Back when there was
Indians?"
    "Oh, my sons. It was
not the ocean that ate the Indians. And
                    it was
not their medicine men who made the ocean
leave. Before I was
a baby even. Before Iowa was
a part of the United States. Or even a
                    state
of mind in a settler. Before man; before
                    words became
language. Long before
Hiroshima dissolved like sugar in your
                    cereal."
    "Huh?"
        "Oh, my neighbors," I whisper
                    because I fear
huge ears and the tongue that may crush me
and my two sons. Oh, my neighbors beyond
                    the gray

moustache, through which a dying father
speaks
"Oh, my neighbors, the giant is eating
very slowly just now. The mountain is
hard. It is not
easy eating. It must be
difficult to live
with an appetite huge as a cloud's. Live
well, my neighbors living still
where all will be green
a little longer. Man
was made to eat.
A little conversation is said
to help
digestion. Laugh. To end
with a reassuringly familiar phrase, make—
and I am serious about this—make
a good meal.

Ralph J. Salisbury

THE ENCUMBRANCE

for Jim Hazard

Man Mountain Potts
the heavyweight champion
of the
Iowa Wrestling
and Plumbers'
Society
is going to pass me on the street.

But he
changes
his mind

and stops
by my right shoulder,
reaches out
and pulls my arm off.

He stuffs it
in my ear.
It comes out my left knee cap
and wiggles its fingers
in B flat.

I smile at Man Mountain
and he lifts me off the pavement
by the chin
and it starts to rain.
I've got to get
more friends,

Just can't make it
through town
anymore.

Dave Kelly

STOPPING NEAR HIGHWAY 80

We are not going to steal the water tower
in Malcom, Iowa,
just stop for a picnic right under it.
Nor need they have removed the lightbulb
in the city park
nor locked the toilet doors.
We are at peace, just eating and drinking
our *poco vino* in Malcom, Iowa,
which evidently once had a band
to go with its bandstand.

We walk down the street, wondering how
it must be to live behind the shades
in Malcom, Iowa, to peer out,
to remember the town as it was before
the Expressway discovered
it, subtracted what would flow
on its river eastwards and westwards.
We are at peace, but when we go into the bar
in Malcom, Iowa, we find that the aunts
and uncles drinking beer have become
monsters and want to hurt us and we do
not know how they could have ever
taken out the giant breasts
of childhood or cooked the fine biscuits
or have told us anything at all
we'd want to know
for living lives as gentle as we can.

David Ray

FOR A SPRING OFFENSIVE

Mostly it is in the skies
the season lives—in the gray
march of the weather's frontiers
over our fields, the low clouds
heavy as hog-dugs and plump,
distended by rain and wind.
Imagine the dirt has mouths
black and involuntary,
needing to be fed something.
Let it be sun or cyclone
—that thing—hail or yellow dust;
let it be either benign
or murderous, so it feeds

the land. For we are the land
and we lie in our hard beds
straining to suck at the clouds
as they blow over, saying:
Make us be grain, weeds, the green
flourishing of the spirit
winter has eaten from us;
make us whatever it is
that grows from earth new-opened.

Robley Wilson, Jr.

THE TOTAL LENGTH
(FOR VALARIE & TOM RAWORTH)

the total length of
the northern Iowa border
from the middle of
the Mississippi channel
to the middle of
the Big Sioux channel measures
268 miles 98 chains and 23 links or
269 miles 461 yards 4 inches
the entrance fee to
Disneyland (package deal) is
$14.15 for each adult
$12.70 for each child
the man from General Pest Control
told us to empty all
shelves & cupboards & not
to enter the house
within 5 hours according to him
the Orientals live
in the basement and are difficult

to get at look my big toe
    has grown real big
      (by Tamsin Hollo)
in 1852 the Boundary Survey expedition
   under Capt. Andrew Talcott of Washington
     consisted of 43 men 14 surveyors
  a doctor a hunter an interpreter
    four cooks chainmen flagmen
      monument builders teamsters
    wood choppers & general handymen
    bands of Sioux
   still ruled the prairies
      buffalo and elk
     CONOCO HOTTEST BRAND GOING

Josephine Clare

IOWA

A life of bottles by the kitchen sink,
lidless mornings sponging up the sun,
night letters in laundromats, afternoons
in watery cafes crouched against the wind.

My images are eating in the east,
dishes growing mold, growing empty,
clean as bone. Mind is what we gum it with
while love comes walking slowly from the west.

Peter Klappert

SPRING PLOWING

East of Omaha, the freshly plowed fields
steam in the night like lakes.
The smell of the earth floods over the roads.
The fieldmice are moving their nests
to the higher ground of fence-rows,
the old among them crying out to the owls
to take them all. The paths in the grass
are loud with the squeak of their carts.
They keep their lanterns covered.

Ted Kooser

IOWA STONE MASON

for Sam

My infant son brings rocks into our house
he lugs enormous stones up from the creek
hordes them under his bed lines them up
At the beach too it is the rocks the stones
the rocks that interest him acres of rocks
he is kicking sorting bringing them home in
grocery sacks ruining his father's shocks

I ask him why he does this: "Because I
like to," says Sam as if to say any fool
can see there is meaning in a rock
There is not a doubt in his mind tonight
he is sleeping with a rock: "Love Rock,"
he calls it he is five years old is Sam
born in Iowa City on April 17, 1969

Sam's great grandfather (on his mother's
side) was an old Iowa stone mason

I met him only once you had the sense
he knew how to hold on to things
wrenches hammer handles rocks crowbars
his tools were in perfect order he lived
in a solid stone house he built himself
Into his eighties he still had all his teeth
his hands were like great slabs of stone

Joe David Bellamy

ON A PAINTING BY PATIENT B OF THE INDEPENDENCE STATE HOSPITAL FOR THE INSANE

I

These seven houses have learned to face one another,
But not at the expected angles. Those silly brown lumps,
That are probably meant for hills and not other houses,
After ages of being themselves, though naturally slow,
Are learning to be exclusive without offending.
The arches and entrances (down to the right out of sight)
Have mastered the lesson of remaining closed.
And even the skies keep a certain understandable distance,
For these are the houses of the very rich.

II

One sees their children playing with leopards, tamed
At great cost, or perhaps it is only other children,
For none of these objects is anything more than a spot,
And perhaps there are not any children but only leopards
Playing with leopards, and perhaps there are only the spots.
And the little maids from the windows hanging like tongues,
Calling the children in, admiring the leopards,
Are the dashes a child might represent motion by means of,
Or dazzlement possibly, the brillance of solid-gold houses.

III

The clouds resemble those empty balloons in cartoons
Which approximate silence. These clouds, if clouds they are
(And not the smoke from the seven aspiring chimneys),
The more one studies them the more it appears
They too have expressions. One might almost say
They have their habits, their wrong opinions, that their
Impassivity masks an essentially lovable foolishness,
And they will be given names by those who live under them
Not public like mountains' but private like companions'.

Donald Justice

THE DIME STORE MAN

Inventory shows
bolts of cloth,
forgeries, breakage,
greasy sacks of change.

Demand and supply,
Laurel and Hardy,
wreck every plan;
the transfer to Phoenix

will never come.
He waits for burglars
chopping through the roof
to blow the safe for petty cash.

Shoppers, browsing,
slip items
under their coats;
he disappears in shrinkage.

Lawrence Kramer

3 from F O R   T H E   I O W A   D E A D

III

Morning Sun, Stone City, Boone, What Cheer:
In the hysteria of history
These names for home rang in the homesick ear,
With the warm sound of friend and family,
Of Iowa, where winter cracks your skull,
Where summer floats on fields, green river flowing,
Where autumn stains your hand with walnut hull,
Spring shakes the land with a loud gust of growing.

But their true season was the one of dying.
Summer, autumn, winter, spring all ran
Into one flaming moment, doomed plane flying,
Sinking ship, exploding shell, edged knife:
For home is not birthplace, but the place a man
Dares a way of death, to keep a way of life.

IV

Most of their life was simply, to make life:
The clover planted and the cattle bred,
Each year the wheat field ripped by the plough's clean knife,
The crust of earth cut like the crust of bread,
The fat hogs slopped, the ludicrous, loud hogs,
The skimmed milk saucered for the lazy cats,
The careful mating of the hunting dogs,
The oat bin plugged against the ravenous rats.

But then their life changed simply, to end lives:
The strange men killed less quickly than the brown
Beef steer by the sledge and the neat knives,
The child's hand begging but without an arm,
The cattle shelled in the defended farm,
The crazed cat shot for luck in the taken town.

VII

Say that in the end their life was one
Quick autumn burning the leaves with their own blood,

Say that they fought so there might be the sun
Over their land, as they died in the mud.
Not from an abstract sense of wrong and right
But for the hill they fenced with aching arm
They went to the unwilled war—and wrote one night,
It's a lousy land and a hell of a way to farm.

Say that for those who came from corn and flock,
By inland rivers where the catfish hang
In the dark pool, and the moccasin hides its fang,
Where the warm milk is cooled in the old gray crock,
It was a tough, hard, bitter death as they sprang
And poured their rich blood over the barren rock.

Paul Engle

A HARD WINTER

It was cold in Iowa
When I was 8
And colder in Asia
My uncle wrote.

I remember the snow
On television and hearing
About frostbite and frozen
Corpses. Combat boots
Vs. tennis shoes.

It's really no colder
Than Iowa but it never
Warms up my uncle wrote.
I never knew it snowed
In Asia and got cold.

I remember waves
Of yellow midgets

In quilted coats
Running dope crazed
Into battle.
And the mud that Spring
Was even worse.

In Des Moines in 1951
We idolized a Marine
We'd heard about
In Korea. He played dead
And the Chinese kicked
Out his teeth
One by one. He didn't move.
They took his clothes
And boots but still
He played dead
In his underwear
In the snow.

The winter of 1951
Was hard all over
The world.

An icicle fell
On Gutch Ellis' head
And Ralphie Benson left
The surface of his tongue
On the flag pole
In the school yard.

It was a bright Thursday
Morning and 5 below zero.

Robert Slater

IOWA DEAD

By the river town
the little old ladies go
down with flowers for the dead
of eight wars, only sixteen
sides that fought
with justice

David Ray

NINE YEARS TODAY

I wash the dandruff off my glasses. All night, farmers talked
of spring plowing in the street. Loudly. Demonstrating the spread
earth with their thick hands. My nose clusters among dead elms,
coughing. Cross-pollination. It has set in on my son's birthday. No
matter where he goes he remembers he was born on the spring plains
of Iowa. Unable in our twenties to take such open land, we lived
next to an alfalfa roasting plant on the edge of town. Such loneliness
we settled for alfalfa. Sweet alfalfa. And high trucks passing through
with their tunnels of dust. All night diesels and pigs squealing in
our veins.

Today he is home. Nine years of searching for a birthday
cake. I hold his hand and rock as I used to rock him at three A.M.
chanting *The Windhover* through the fierce dark of his first year
pain. Cross-pollination. Happy Birthday America! I love you. I
love you, and the frail eagles of your hands.

John Judson

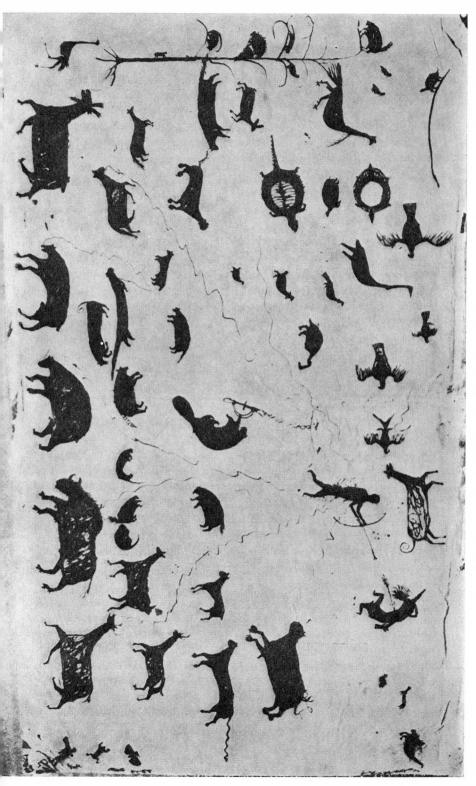

PICTOGRAPH, *Wacochachi*

On one sheet there is a sign for a river, a wavy line going north-south on the page. Two Indians are pictured riding on horses, which are running, and one is shooting a buffalo with bow and arrow. The Indians are pictured on the left side of the river, which is probably the Mississippi, and best interpretation seems to be that they traveled northward on the west bank of the river (the fork at the end of the river line showing direction traveled). They rode horses and shot a buffalo while their horses ran alongside . . .

The time is spring, indicated by many clues: a pelican with a knob on its beak, something it has only in spring; a prairie chicken strutting as it does in its spring courtship dance; moose, elk and deer with short antlers. A female deer is shown with "scrambled" insides. a pictographic convention denoting, among other things, that the animal is pregnant, as in fairly early spring. Trees are leafless. A tadpole is depicted, and a frog. A butterfly is out; a dragon fly out or emerging.

A beaver is shown in a steel trap, a popular article of trade goods since the white man's traps were more effective than any the Indians had. Beaver were usually trapped in the spring, when the pelts were prime and transportation by water to the trading post was easy, or when an itinerant trader might be expected to be making his rounds soon. The set shown is a typical drowning set, with a float stick like those still used by beaver trappers.

Spring hunts were customary among Indians of the region. The hunters would go out in small groups, hunting and trapping, and return with a supply of furs and skins to trade. All evidence within the pictograph suggests that this is the record of such a hunt—the signs showing spring, the beaver being trapped, and the variety of animals shown as having been taken by the hunters. This abundance of wildlife and the good hunting and trapping are clearly shown on one sheet of the pictograph, with a buffalo hunt and fishing exploits on the other.

Lines connect the figure of one Indian with a variety of pictures indicating he got the animals pictured, and still others are shown upside down—dead. Besides the buffalo shot from running horses, animals taken and shown by the connecting line include lynx (short tail and claws shown), mountain lion (longer tail), bull elk, buffalo, black bear, otter (upside down also), grizzly bear (its claws more prominent), timber wolf, moose (the "bell" of the bull moose clearly drawn), possibly a fisher (upside down), rabbit, snapping turtle, a flying bird with banded tail which may be a golden eagle, and another flying bird with a forked tail which may be a swallow-tailed kite, a kind of hawk formerly found on rare occasions along the Mississippi in Iowa. Animals shown upside down, or dead, include muskrat, skunk, mink, raccoon, possum, the otter (connected with line), timber wolf (connected with line), fox, and an animal that is possibly a fisher (connected with line).

A row of animals shown right side up were probably animals observed but not taken by the hunters. Below the mountain lion is a buck deer and to the left of it a doe; and above the dead animals, reading from right to left, an animal which may be a fawn, a wolverine, woodchuck, badger and probably a cat of some kind. Besides the snapping turtle, the hunting half of the pictograph on the right also shows a soft-shelled turtle and the ordinary hard-shelled turtle. Other birds include: two more hawks—one large, perhaps an eagle, one small—a crane, a ruffed grouse, a strutting prairie chicken and a quail. A bird in front of them is probably a goose or swan. Another crane is shown in a corner. A strutting turkey gobbler is near the tree, and above it are a jacksnipe and a woodcock.

In the tree are possum, squirrel, marten, porcupine and grouse, and a chipmunk running up the tree. In the corner behind the elk are a butterfly, a frog and an unidentified figure. In another corner is a mouse, a weasel and an unidentified bird; and in the corner above the tree, a turtle crawling on a bank.

The lynx at far right, connected to the man with a line, is shown running, and with lines emerging from its mouth, a pictographic convention for sound or screaming. The apparent meaning is that the lynx screamed, charged, and was killed by the hunter while in the act of charging.

As for the hunter himself, he is shown without any hair at all, as was common among the Sauk Indians who had a village on the Rock River in Illinois not far from Colonel Davenport's trading post. He carries a bow, with an arrow ready to shoot, and lines on his lower back are probably intended to represent bow case and quiver.

He has just shot a man, using only one arrow—a man who carries a clearly-drawn flintlock rifle and is shown running. The man shot is not a white man, since whites were commonly depicted wearing hats. Two interpretations are possible for the hair style of this man with a rifle. An old person is sometimes pictured this way, but more often this type of hair represents an Ojibway. Since the hunters were probably traveling north, an encounter with a less-than-friendly Ojibway would appear a logical explanation. In some cases, too, the term "Ojibway" has been used to describe any or all enemies; the man with the rifle may, therefore, be merely an enemy of some unnamed tribe.

Whoever the slain man was, the feat of killing him with just one arrow, while he carried a gun, would be a noteworthy achievement, one to be especially remembered and making that particular spring hunt more memorable. The hunter has used one arrow, the reversed barb at the end of the second one perhaps indicating a magic arrow or perhaps meaning "I used just one arrow."

The sheet of the pictograph on the left, which includes the buffalo hunt, deals mostly with fishing. The line which goes through the buffalo is a typical sign for a journey on a stream, and the fork at the end the common way of depicting that this is the direction of travel.

Fish shown at the right of the buffalo are wall-eyed pike, sucker, spoonbill catfish (which is found only in the Mississippi and Missouri Rivers and their larger tributaries), and above the men, a perch. Two men are shown in a canoe, the man in the stern paddling and the one in the bow, standing and spearing a fish. The pictograph shows tines of the spear. The canoe has upswept ends, indicating a birch bark canoe typical of the north country rather than the dugouts used by the Sac and Fox Indians further downstream.

In the corner near the men, a creature is shown swimming, with "sound" lines coming from its head. Best interpretation seems to be that this is a loon. Its "pigeon-toed" feet are indicated far back on its body and it does indeed sometimes swim under water by using its wings for propulsion, as shown in the pictograph.

Below the speared fish is a comment on the quality of life—there were lots of little bugs. Below that is a coiled snake with its mouth open, and below that what is probably another open-mouthed snake, swimming or crawling. The big fish just to the left of the bugs is a sturgeon. The biggest fish in the pictograph, near the center, is probably a muskellunge or a northern pike. Ignoring for the moment the bird connected to the man, there are three more birds shown, all water birds: a heron with a fish, a pelican, and a swan. At the edge of the paper, a cow buffalo can be seen. Below are a frog and tadpole and what is probably a toad; near the swan is an unidentified small animal. Near the corner a small animal with a long tail, probably a squirrel, is making a lot of noise, after the manner of squirrels.

Along the bank at the bottom of the sheet, perhaps sitting on a log, is a row of turtles, and just to the left of them a somewhat conventionalized dragon fly. From the number of legs shown on the dragon fly, this may be a nymph stage of the insect rather than adult, indicating it is emerging.

A man is shown seated on the bank, fishing with a pole, something the Indian learned from the white man. He's fishing in a stream, as indicated by the many wavy lines below him, and in the stream are sheephead or fresh water drum, crappie, a bass he has hooked, sunfish and bullhead. Above him are channel catfish (forked tail), flathead catfish (blunt nose and nearly square tail), fresh water drum, and buffalo fish. Next to these fish, a dogfish and a gar, and behind the fisherman a crane, a spoonbill catfish, and on the bank a ground squirrel sits by its hole watching. Below the ground squirrel, a coiled line may be an indication of time elapsed during the trip, more than two months.

Along the lefthand edge, two men are shown fishing with hand lines, as the Indians often did, and using frogs for bait. One of these men also has a bow case and quiver. One unidentified fish is shown. Behind the figure on horseback is another bird, not identified, an unidentified figure on an angled line, and what is probably another tree.

Again on this sheet, the Indians are shown with no hair. This may be significant, since customarily the Sauks, or Sacs, and Foxes plucked out their hair leaving, at most, a scalp lock. Use of turtles and muskrats, as well as methods of fishing, also suggest the pictograph may be the work of a Sauk Indian, or perhaps a member of the Fox clan, since by this time the two groups were living together, as they do now.

In the center of the sheet, an Indian with bow case and quiver is shown standing behind a tree, using a gun to shoot another man. This man and the hand-line fishermen also appear to be wearing leggings. Behind the man with the gun, a row of dots indicates a long trail; he has followed the man he shot, probably for a long time and long distance, and then hid behind the tree and shot him. A line is attached to the top of this man's head, and at the other end of the line is a bird, a typical way of depicting a man's personal totem or identification, with a line coming from the top of his head or from his mouth. In this case, the bird identifying the man in the pictograph gives rise to some interesting speculation, since it is a small black bird with a banded tail and carries another very small bird in one foot. The best explanation seems to be that the bird is a hawk, and the black coloration, banded tail and small bird in its talons suggest a bird now known as a pigeon hawk but formerly known as a black sparrow hawk.

Jack and Mary Musgrove

BLACK HAWK IN HIDING

Everyone can see me standing in the center
of the stockade, which I hear was built to contain
white soldiers who got drunk or disobeyed
their officers—now it houses their prisoners of war.
The soldiers grow sober looking at us
in the sunlight over the fence.

*

A chain runs around my wrists and under my balls.
It circles both my legs like an iron vine.
A black bar is fastened to both feet
to make certain I won't run far,
and I don't try, I just stand still.

*

I hope I will die soon
so I can go into the woods around Rock River
and stop knee-deep among the mesh
of creepers growing under the trees,
and breathe the brown bittersweet stink
of stale fish and grass, keeping back
in the wet shade where no one can see me.

George Keithley

IN DREAM: THE PRIVACY OF SEQUENCE

always expecting the winter
to be a sad one
i slept after heavy eating of food
and waited until the portions
grew alive.
they sprouted antlers and formed

into circles,
fitted themselves perfectly
into my hollow teeth
and spoke to each other
in comfort about the quiet welcome
they were to receive:
of imitating the distance
between the sky, earth
and the children
shaping a figure from the snow,
recognized and visible
in the eyes of old people
quickly running to their trunks
and fires,
unrolling the contracted faces
of relatives:
long trails of smoke streamed out
from the houses that rested
deep inside the hills.
trees stood about with their arms
stretched out over their foreheads
blocking out the sun,
wondering why the children's laughter
at that moment
seemed to cover everything
in the whole valley including sound.
the trees turned to the old man
who had been sitting in front
of the sun.
the old man right away thought
he knew the reason why the trees' eyes
closed when he met them with his.
repositioning himself, he pretended
to gaze out past them
into the valley.
relieved, he whistled like a bird
and then suddenly realized
much more the quietness

that was in the air.
without birds or leaves
or anything to travel in the wind with
except his acknowledgement
which went from tree to tree
being refused at each ear.
feeling strange, he stood up
and saw for the first time
children running in the open
with kites in their hands.
the old man was familiar
with the faces in the sky
and once in his dream
these were actually disguised gods,
infected birds who lowered
their guts to the mouths of children.

outside, the depicted visitor
standing as the weather
gathers itself around me
holding in each hand
strings of dried hearts,
the coming hardship of death.
with a mouthfull of ashes,
he digs into the earth
hoping to save his warmth
for the dog who sleeps without dreams
or without me to stand above him,
reminding him of the cold
and the dark thin birds
inside my stomach.
his memory of blood tied in little bags.

forgetting the good
of the coming spring,
my fingernails grew long
like brittle shovels
and dug out the squirrel
and pheasant from my teeth,
thick and warm, resembling rocks.

afraid of the daylight
they only came out halfway
from the earth.
i wanted to protect them.
i thought only of their outcome.
i thought of ways to deceive
the dark thin birds speckled
through the sky, wearing masks.
i thought that whoever took
to their air would eventually
stop in flight and then decay,
afraid that it would be my
own howling that i would hear
out in the open
mixed with the talking of deer.
the deer who sometimes laugh
while skinning a man after a day's hunt.
their fingers poking through the path
of the bullet, tracing the clot.
the head left behind for the people
in the woods.

i found myself between the airs
of changing weather
unable to distinguish
what to kill, layers of wind over my eyes,
growing old and uncertain,
cutting out the kneeling children
linked together by arms
and thrown to the dog
who refuses though he knows
it is a worship to his skill
and lets the others eat.
once, a boy with puffed-up eyes
took out the roof of his mouth
and sharpened his knife
on his heart,
licked the knife and smiled,
carved me a boat
with arms and legs.

all night, the boat struggled to lift
its burnt belly to the stars.
sensing that the boy had fallen asleep,
daylight came,
took the boy's knife and sliced
off the boy's fingers,
crushed them, dried and sifted them
with its hands and breath
until they were trees.
the particles that blew away
from the daylight's warm breath
made the boy dream
that he had rubbed his hands
against the sky.

Ray A. Young Bear

POWWOW

They all see the same movies.
    They shuffle on one leg,
        Scuffing the dust up,
    Shuffle on the other.
They are all the same:
    A Sioux dance to the spirits;
    A war dance by four Chippewa;
    A Dakota dance for rain;
        We wonder why we came.
Even tricked out in the various braveries—
    Black buffalo tassels, beadwork, or the brilliant
    Feathers at the head, at the buttocks—
Even in long braids and the gaudy face-paints,
        They all dance with their eyes turned
    Inward—like a woman nursing
A sick child she already knows

Will die. For the time, she nurses it,
All the same. The loudspeakers shriek;
    We leave our bleacher seats to wander
    Among the wikiups and lean-tos
In search for hot dogs. The Indians
    Are already packing; have
    Resumed green dungarees and khaki—
Castoff combat issues of World War II.
    (Only the Iroquois do not come here—
They work in structural steel; they have a contract
    Building the United Nations
    And Air Force installations for our future wars.)
These, though, have dismantled their hot-dog stand
    And have to drive all night
To jobs in truck stops and all-night filling stations.
    We ask directions and
    They scuttle away from us like moths.
    Past the trailers,
    Beyond us, one tepee is still shining
Over all the rest. Inside, circled by a ring
    Of children, in the glare
    Of one bare bulb, a shrunken fierce-eyed man
Squats at his drum, all bones and parchment,
    While his dry hands move
    On the drumhead, always drumming, always
Raising his toothless drawn jaw to the light
    Like a young bird drinking, like a chained dog,
Howling his tribe's song for the restless young
    Who wander in and out.
    Words of such great age,
Not even he remembers what they mean.
    We tramp back to our car,
    Then nearly miss the highway, squinting
Through red and yellow splatterings on the windshield—
    The garish and beautiful remains
    Of grasshoppers and dragonflies
That go with us; that do not live again.

W. D. Snodgrass

THE PLACE OF V

a short day has grown
into the sky,
balancing itself
between our places
of breathing.
the thought of warm
roomlight has left me.
the thought of our
hands against the house,
measuring each corner
and window has left me.
snow melts on the ground.
corn appears in the eyes
of thin birds.
the food you left
for the wandering man
walks behind you.
the killer's car
sits under the sun.
its eyes skim over
the walls of a house
looking for signs that
will make it remember
but it doesn't find
anything except
the thought of a boy
carrying a boy who keeps
on fainting, falling
into seizures.
from the fog an old man
troubles his weak legs
to kick the stones alive.
his moist face attracts
you, tells you to leave
the past alone.
you offer the comfort

of your finger to fit
around his finger
now that he is walking
away in his father's
hands in the form
of four sticks.

Ray A. Young Bear

HE IS BURNING

He is burning
to see her, his eyes
are smeared with smoke.
The flame in his flesh

a torchlight which leads
the man home. Four days
on horse from the hunting camp,
the thin huts hung with skins—

unlike those long houses
built of elm bark
in the village where she sleeps
among so many women.

At night now he sees
the meadow of her brown eyes,
her breasts blossom
above the bent grass—

He is burning to hold her
close the way the wind
holds fire in a bush
until it eats down to the dirt.

But by dawn
he hears the whole town
waking—a dozen
or more dogs barking—

Barking at the dawn!
Rides in to find the fields
wild with horses, his hogs
driven from their pen.

The lodges are lit like kindling
for cooking. Fire consumes
all the frames. Walls fly up
as if to outleap their flames.

Men as white as ice
are chasing the children out
of the village to mingle
among the hogs,

the women wading after
in a surf of skirts
and grass, struck
across the back with sticks—

He is burning
to bury his knife
in the breast of the blond lieutenant
leading the raiding party,

who withdraw to their fort
not far from the mouth
of the shrieking river—

Behind them a hundred homes
of the bark of black elms
blazed to the ground
as a precaution
against contamination.

Stragglers return from the fields
and while they gather
the wind weaves the hair
of young and old together

and weaves the braids of water
flowing by their feet—
the river where they see
their faces floating away.

George Keithley

ARROWHEADS

"there are no more arrowheads in Peterson, Iowa"
—A FRIEND

a century ago
there were plenty
you could watch them being
fashioned from
a piece of flint
pulled from the heart
of a three-point buck
but now they're locked
in glass cases, next to
an Indian skeleton
lost in grandma's cedar chest
hocked in pawnshops
boarded up years ago

Mark Johnson

POEM TO BE READ AT 3 A.M.

Excepting the diner
On the outskirts
The town of Ladora
At 3 A.M.
Was dark but
For my headlights
And up in
One second-story room
A single light
Where someone
Was sick or
Perhaps reading
As I drove past
At seventy
Not thinking
This poem
Is for whoever
Had the light on

Donald Justice

ALL MORNING

All morning a wren has been building
a nest in my ear. I will shelter anyone

who needs it, it's always been
my problem, & who can resist small

birds? They cannot hurt you,
even their tail feathers

twitching like soft razor blades,
my friend, oh, my friend.

Terry Stokes

LIVING TOGETHER

It is nearly spring in Iowa.
Already I have inherited
a soggy garden and a cat
named Virginia Woolf
and gossipy neighbors
poking noses through
curtains like crocuses
through the thin uncertain chill
of early March. I admit we look
suspicious. I pretend you live
in a Paris garret and I am
your small slant-eyed mistress.

For years I detested just
what I enjoy most now.
For breakfast I make eggs
and threaten
to drown the whole midwest
in pepper. Marketing,
we slide down the aisles, giggly
as newlyweds sniffing and squeezing
plums. When you leave the house
I celebrate my privacy,
the luxury of it, I am free
as laundry blown loose
from the lines. Still,
I distrust this easy
domesticity,
though I have opened myself
to you, a cautious guest
risking a reckless visit.

In a week
when I fly back to
the Vermont winter,
I fear I may close
and lose myself in books

and other men and the casual
love I fall out of and out of.
Pitching myself
into the open air, shuttling
across season and distance is
as simple as turning on one elbow
and reaching across the mattress,
this lazy afternoon, to touch you.

Jane Shore

CEDAR RAPIDS IN THE MORNING

The light from the river lies brightly sober
On your books, the hot plate that wouldn't work,
The bottle of Port we didn't finish.

Without my glasses, I cannot read the titles,
But, here and there, I recognize a dust jacket.

Nothing sounds reasonable except a cup of tea
In an empty lunch room across this quiet town.

But I do not disturb your rest.
Somewhere, there is a train I know I will never catch.

R. R. Cuscaden

ON A REPLY TO COMPLAINTS OF AIR POLLUTION

the mayor of cedar rapids was the one
who said smells mean work

well bill said oh work means smells
and maurice said mean work smells
and jim said work smells mean
and rita said mean smells work

and sister scholastica
she said wow smells work mean

John Knoepfle

THE PICNIC

It is the picnic with Ruth in the spring.
Ruth was third on my list of seven girls
But the first two were gone (Betty) or else
Had someone (Ellen has accepted Doug).
Indian Gully the last day of school;
Girls make the lunches for the boys too.
I wrote a note to Ruth in algebra class
Day before the test. She smiled, and nodded.
We left the cars and walked through the young corn
The shoots green as paint and the leaves like tongues
Trembling. Beyond the fence where we stood
Some wild strawberry flowered by an elm tree
And Jack-in-the-pulpit was olive ripe.
A blackbird fled as I crossed, and showed
A spot of gold or red under its quick wing.
I held the wire for Ruth and watched the whip
Of her long, striped skirt as she followed.
Three freckles blossomed on her thin, white back

Underneath the loop where the blouse buttoned.
We went for our lunch away from the rest,
Stretched in the new grass, our heads close
Over unknown things wrapped up in wax papers.
Ruth tried for the same, I forget what it was,
And our hands were together. She laughed,
And a breeze caught the edge of her little
Collar and the edge of her brown, loose hair
That touched my cheek. I turned my face in-
to the gentle fall. I saw how sweet it smelled.
She didn't move her head or take her hand.
I felt a soft caving in my stomach
As at the top of the highest slide
When I had been a child, but was not afraid,
And did not know why my eyes moved with wet
As I brushed her cheek with my lips and brushed
Her lips with my own lips. She said to me
Jack, Jack, different than I had ever heard,
Because she wasn't calling me, I think,
Or telling me. She used my name to
Talk in another way I wanted to know.
She laughed again and then she took her hand;
I gave her what we both had touched—can't
Remember what it was, and we ate the lunch.
Afterward we walked in the small, cool creek
Our shoes off, her skirt hitched, and she smiling,
My pants rolled, and then we climbed up the high
Side of Indian Gully and looked
Where we had been, our hands together again.
It was then some bright thing came in my eyes,
Starting at the back of them and flowing
Suddenly through my head and down my arms
And stomach and my bare legs that seemed not
To stop in feet, not to feel the red earth
Of the Gully, as though we hung in a
Touch of birds. There was a word in my throat
With the feeling and I knew the first time
What it meant and I said, it's beautiful.

Yes, she said, and I felt the sound and word
In my hand join the sound and word in hers
As in one name said, or in one cupped hand.
We put back on our shoes and socks and we
Sat in the grass awhile, crosslegged, under
A blowing tree, not saying anything.
And Ruth played with shells she found in the creek,
As I watched. Her small wrist which was so sweet
To me turned by her breast and the shells dropped
Green, white, blue, easily into her lap,
Passing light through themselves. She gave the pale
Shells to me, and got up and touched her hips
With her light hands, and we walked down slowly
To play the school games with the others.

John Logan

HEARING THE MORNING NEWS

Dear friends—I dream familiar
rooms, and people dancing on sand.
Wake up to news from Iowa:

"Mother and child
killed in a storm.
Ankeny torn apart."

In Des Moines, bicycles rust;
your yard is green mirage.
Here, it is the same, rain;

roses wild; profuse in neglect.
The screened porch damp and cool
like cabins at camp in evergreens.

Remember Marquette winters?
Those heightened evenings found
in that isolate, old town—

your young marriage, new daughter,
pup that chewed your bed, unending
fjords of Freshman themes.

. . . ten years since we watched
northern geese seek some distance
through a far stream of sky. Now,

networks and interstates keep us
separate . . . yet, today you are
presences—prompt like the news. .

See us then, when we ate together;
that stew we shared, important
as love.

Izora Corpman

DAS EWIG-WEIBLICHE

A woman waiting in the cab
Of a pick-up truck in town today
Observes her man and others talk
Of corn and hogs, and feed and hay,
And drift into the Railroad Bar.
She settles back with time to kill,
Sheer resignation in the way
Her arm lies on the window sill.

Ernest Kroll

HIGH SOCIETY, IOWA CITY, IOWA

"Ever art thou dancing in battle.
Never was beauty like thine, as,
with thy hair flowing about thee
thou dost ever dance, a naked
warrior upon the breast of Siva."
—HINDU SONG TO KALI

Peter Cooley lives on Dodge Street south,
with his wife, Jacqueline, and small daughter.
Although a walkable distance away, I drive.
My white VW bus rolls down the street,
an intractable tank, impervious to degrees. Snipers
see me coming, shoot, run for cover. The twin guns
over my head-lights shatter their black frocks.
Diplomas batter my windows and doors, converge
on my tires. I accelerate to thirty-five, ignore
the light, turn to the children with small knives,
sharp teeth, spray their faces through the trees. Coming
to a stop, a small conflict with a Doberman Pinscher
and a ten-foot whip. I run up the steps, knock, Peter answers.
Bursting through the room, I see Nicole, the daughter,
rising. My mind is as one that dances. Machetes
drop from her hands like wild petals.

Stephen Dobyns

MOUNT PLEASANT, U.S.A.

at night
I'm a man surprising himself
in sleep a slight stirring of the curtains
at the window the flies kiss
the bottles to their heart's content
the glass
is stiff with their chanting

       each night I shift
    to another place
    to another failure
in Iowa I dream of Nanjangud

                  my mother
the illiterate waiting
her eyes gone dim her hair
           off to nowhere . . .

given up on sons given up on herself
waiting the night for the day
to be over for the day to begin

         in the bars
of Chicago in the scowl
of Mount Pleasanteans in the handshake
of friends in the flashback
of promises in my exile

the cage I carry is the cage I made

G. S. Sharat Chandra

TO THE MAD GARDENER OF SOLON

   Roar One
It is easier to plant dreams
when they are vegetables,
and easier to handle women
when they all smell like old fish.
I am earth and water
and fire and soul. You stick
your image into me, and I take it.

I mimic it and squeeze it into shape.
Then I am the garden you plant in.

I am omnipresent. I devour all.
I devour your seed. I understand you.
I say "plant," "invest," "conquer,"
and lay myself back in a ditch.
Earth taste sweetens your mouth
but you dream of shoveling
yourself under.

Roar Two

Here I come smelling of old wife.
You run scattering your garden tools.
You run until you come to the bar of your dreams
where a mother serves beer, and a grandmother
says "yes, have another."

You call women soft: they give everything they got.
But she is with me, and she gives destruction.

I must be ten feet tall
with thorns. You tear me down limb by limb. I persist.

We come to know each other so well, only
to give tools for the fight.

Spray me down, hoe me down.
Let the systemic poison you buy
for yourself, or the herbicide
you buy to chop me down, cling
like a Medea's cape to your vegetables.
In order to rid yourself of me,
you yourself must become poisonous.

Susan Zwinger

SHARON CENTER, IOWA

"Some years the ground pulls harder . . ."
—DON SCHOTT

He mounts his tractor.
There are creatures in trees
Whose names I do not know.
There are others in procession before us.
Pigs the size of buffalo Cattle
The tails and markings of horses.
Iowa. What am I doing in Iowa?
Ann lies in the sun. Dozing. Depressed.
Stripping, rising on my hind legs,
Hairy, cloven-footed,
Centaur, I declare myself/Centaur.
Then chicken. Then horse. Bull. Then pig.
She too—Centaur. Then chicken. Horse. Bull. Then pig.
Let us plant our dreams.
Write them down and plant them.
Plant sugar cubes
Make love
Then dig it up/turn it over
And plant the ground
That ground we made love on.
What will grow there?
Rhubarb.
A peach tree.
The ground holds me as I make love to it.
How is it birds no longer fly?
Horses only. The entire state of Iowa.
What about deities
These deities that eat your brains?
And why anyway should I mind that?
I am busy planting my brains.
I will harvest them remind me please before leaving.
The time has come.
O look Centaur Snowing Your eyes

Your eyes
They touch me
I have been asleep.
Does it hurt?

Robert Sward

CONVERSATION IN THE ELITE CAFÉ

(from 7½ Cents)

"Was you to the dance last night out at the Royal?"
says the waitress, talking through her nose.
"I was there, was you?" says a milk truck driver
likewise.
"Yeah, I was there. I never seen you though."
"Well I never seen you neither."
"That's funny, I was there."
"Well, I never seen you."
"Where was you at? I never seen you."
"Well, it's funny we never seen each other."

Richard Bissell

OLD DUBUQUE

*There is no past, present and future time
here in Dubuque, there is just Dubuque time.*
—RICHARD BISSELL

From Grant's grave Galena
we drove down in a daze
(from two days of antiques)
to the Mississippi,

then crossed over at noon
to old, hunchbacked Dubuque:
a never-say-die town,
a gray, musty pawnshop,
still doing business; while
on the bluff, blue jeans flap
in a river wind laced
with fresh paint and dead carp.

We couldn't find the house
where she once lived and died
(at ninety, baking bread)
somewhere in the hard maze
of crusty shops and streets.
And Dubuque is a spry,
goofy-sad river gal,
lost in a patchwork haze
of tears and years gone by;
and I love this mad place
like my dead grandmother
loved her steins of Star beer.

Dave Etter

HARRY JAMES & THE UNTUNED PIANO

Harry it's a great thrill to shake that mitt
    here in The Hawkeye State I've shaken
    the Count's the Duke's the fabulous Louis
    Bellson's from little Moline on the river
    but this is an honor a kick
    I can't tell you

Thank you it's nice

And the folks Harry they loved you out there
    all the old tunes Carnegie Hall
    You Made Me Love You
    Harry too bad about that piano Harry

Aw man

I don't suppose over the years Helen O'Connell
    Vegas Betty Grable you bump into
    what's the word I want Harry

Aw man when a fine piano player like
    you know Jack sits down

No kidding I'll bet that fried the band
    for a loop those pickled notes
    you practice much Harry
    work out I mean on last week's
    show we talked with the great

I practice sure I practice

I'll bet you had to scrap some numbers
    change the book hubba hubba
    Harry what about Hollywood

Look I've got a sore tooth
    can the radio audience see these gums
    the people loved us we play for the people

I ached for you Harry I hurt
    is this your first time
    through Iowa Harry

Once a year the people love us
    popcorn catfish bad pianos
    you roll with the punch
    a nice crowd small but nice

I'll bet this trip is embedded
    Harry how's Jack
    I'll bet he's beer & cold cuts Harry

Listen that particular box was
    I'll tell you about bad boxes
    I mean stinko fella that was a *good*
    OK piano baby very nice

How about getting started Harry
    your big break Betty
    the kids our listeners

I was playing baseball

Baseball Harry

Beaumont Texas American Legion
    we play for the people
    hockey marbles hotdogs
    name your poison
    we play for the people

Gary Gildner

I CONDUCT BEETHOVEN

It is spring in Iowa. I plant my speakers in the fields and conduct
with my feet deep in soil. Birds are puzzled by this flapping forty-
year-old scarecrow. They fly past. Before me our farmhouse is an
orchestra swaying, released from silence. I am a brilliant, graceful
conductor. My stereo orchestra plays with or without me. It plays
when I wave my arms furiously. It plays when I pause to think of
the letter you have sent me. Dear Ludwig, you have written, mocking
my despair.

In bed I told you stories about Beethoven. Your letter says you have tasted the tip of freedom and want to swallow it whole. They say that when he was forty and rejected by Therese Amalfatti (he had proposed marriage), Beethoven never really dared to love again. With my arms locked around your breasts I pitied the older Beethoven. Yes, from the trough of his misery came the late quartets. But what is eternity compared to a farmhouse from day to day? I prefer old Bach, you whispered. And we dove on each other looking for children.

Once inside you I practiced Beethoven. The end of the "Eroica" is no easy lay. You were best at the fourth piano concerto, coming ferociously, straining for twins. The ninth, we laughed, was beyond us both. It is only for those who can love well beyond forty. Stopping between movements I wipe my brow. You tell me that married to yourself you have found your true home. When love dies clichés are cultured pearls and poetry as pretty as cow pie. My favorite clichés are those told about Beethoven: The music is all sex. And only because he was deaf. And he who truly understands the music can never know unhappiness again. You were very unhappy you say and advise me to advise the eldest never to have children.

There are pigs and piglets loose in the purple spring fields of Iowa. The eldest sits on the porch and applauds me as the youngest, on the lawn, rolls over and over. The hogs that root at my feet are pink, black, orange, and gray. They are amazed, bemused by this twitching piece of premature corn. You are free as laundry blown loose from the line, you write me, and advise the youngest to be a child forever. Raising my baton to the wind, I conduct Beethoven.

Bernard Kaplan

CRESTON

On a clear June day
In Creston, Iowa
Everything looks out
Through everything, the doubt

That nature can go on
Ridiculous as when
Da Vinci learned to see
A clear transparency
On earth when Raphael
Saw but the pit of Hell
Or Heaven—and one glance
Opened the Renaissance.

E. L. Mayo

ONLY THE DREAMER CAN CHANGE THE DREAM

Riding on his bike
in the fall
or spring Fel-
lini-like twilight
or dawn, the boy
                    is moved in some way
he does not understand.
A huge grey or green, long porched house
(he's partly color-blind)
crowns a low hill: rise-
s silent as a ship does
before him.
The vision makes him yearn
inside himself. It makes him mourn.
So he cries
            as he rides
                        about the town.
He knows there are other great homes
and other beautiful streets
nearby. But they are not his.
He turns back.
                He gets off his bike

and picks
    up three fragments of unfinished pine
adrift on the green
            (or grey) lawn
thinking—hoping—that perhaps
there is something some place he can fix.

John Logan

THE BAGLEY IOWA POEM

1.
Bagley meant to be
a railroad town
but the railroad
hadn't heard.

Three churches
poulticed
600 people.
(five ninety-nine
after I ran away.)

The sneaky holy-roller summer—
with Christian Endeavor
serving as the dating bureau—
on Main street sat the Methodist madam.

God's sparrow
never flew in our trees
and the angling birch
filling my window
turned into a creaking skeleton
when I became
homesick at home.

2.

No was a great big
thousand letter word
and the consequences
were plenty.

Yes was love
and all that
meant, soured
and scourged
with unhappy knots
that tied the men
to their women
and the women
to their men
and the land
heaved and buckled
and produced
2¢ a bushel
    corn
and separate rooms.

3.

Bagley,
well, yes,
heaved on winter streets,
sweltered in the summer.
Grandma Plummer,
deaf as a post
hole,
traded the attic
for a double-carpeted
dining room
two husbands later.
I don't think I
was through with weddings
before I began but
the illustrations
were out of focus

and the hills
were full of accidents
and proposals.

4.
I fly back to my childhood
trying to get the water-tower
shape right. Shaped like a—

I sneak up on it through the trees,
the apple trees that are young
and shapely. Shaped like—

There on its long spindly legs,
the fat tub of a water-tower
towers over the splattered town

shaped like a great bruise
with the welts running like
mainstreet and over it the water tower

shaped like a Roman candle
waiting to go off if only
someone would set a match to it.

I bring my torch. Water
tower shaped like Canaveral.
Over and over I have dreamed
of seeing Bagley from the moon.

5.
Learning that the town has no more trains
                or buses
shouldn't matter to me who will never go there
                again but
it has put me standing on a corner
under the bus stop sign
in my new graduation suit
and a hat with a flowing scarf

of a color I can't remember
but the dust is blowing—
gum wrappers mince down the street
making their small journey—
and I am headed away.

Ann Darr

ECLOGUES

where I lived the river
        lay like a blue wrist
between the bluffs & the islands
were tiny unctions of green. where
        every morning the horses outside
my house woke the sun & their breath
was like wet foliage
        in the cool air. but in my house
my bedroom poised
        between shadow & light & the light
was flawed by angles of glass
till night disappeared in a moment
        of wonder. the farm fed
on the full hillsides & sheets
of grain seemed to fall
        almost to the river's shore.
but from my window the farm
        was less real: the river & at noon
the fish I could almost hear fading
in its cool depths distracted
        the boy of twelve. my brother
beside me
slept. he was oldest & duty
has deliberate solitude: even my sisters

kept their dolls
    quietly.

the second son: his father
is silent. whose hands are fouled
    with the birth of a new foal & the brother
fixes the blanket
over the mare's belly. the blood! & the younger
    boy thinks the flesh
a burden & at fault
    for its own pain. the others
lift the foal & pull
the small genital till it flexes
with full life.
    I stood in the barn
born second of God's beasts
    & alone in the days of my making.

my grandfather's God
guided him to the river & the Holy
    Ghost, he said, hung
like a white hand over this hill. our farm
    was his & when he died
my father (his son) worked a stone
in the shape of a bird, wings
    upraised as if startled
by my grandfather's death.

my name came from the river
the Fox call "Father" &
    "Source" as if a man's semen
were the only cause & my mother's fluid
    a mere aspiration. my mother
told of monsters who may
have died in the river-bed & she read
    that ice a mile high once
moved over their bones. at night
    the river with cold friction

pushes my slumbering flesh
    & my manhood moves
new
& in its own seed.

my father
    died, feeder of many horses & so fine
an ear he had
he heard the birds with feathered weight
    drop between the green rows
of corn. a gothic
man knowing
no wisdom & in that field we
    no longer plant. the birds
forever float
    above his grave & the ground
gives
more each year.

that winter the farm
    dozed, its tillage deep
in snow. the river
backs a cruel spine against
    the bluffs & boyhood's
dim fish ride
up under the ice, Mother:
    your children. inside
the fire rubs
itself for warmth & the windows
go white with frost.

Dennis Schmitz

MY FATHER'S TRUNK

The soft grainy light of our attic opened
my father's past a little way. His trunk was
a place where years were shut in him like the leaves
of a book whose title alone he displayed
—I wondered if it was mostly about love,
though other strengths were there pressing a vision
on my landscape. I loved the hunters riding
in coontail caps through the ornamental path
inside the lid—I knew by heart the clipping
how he bagged a timber wolf in some woods near
Farley, Iowa, and I sported the brass
knuckles and dangled the billyclub of his
sheriff days, I aimed the elegant pistol
at spider targets—the topmost color in my
first spectrum was the greenpearl of the handle.
Under the sulphur whiteshirts with hard collars
and their beautiful musty smell and the old
leather smell of razorstrop were keys to locks
I never could open; an oval locket,
sealed tight as a dream, carried I always thought
my mother's image. I tried never to laugh
at the ohio matchbox with the sewing
kit of his bachelor days, and though it was
hard to picture the big fingers threading a
needle, I once saw that hand lift a bluebell
from its tower and twirl it like a sparkler.
The letter in the blue envelope he had
never opened bore a script daintier than
my mother's exquisite flourish, and when I
left the blue flap sealed, ordinary breathing
avowed the silence but did not disturb it.
Stale flower smell on another clipping brushed
me like rain: "a knot of English violets
enhanced the heliotrope gown" his bride wore
at their winter wedding, before "a long tour."
And every solitary honeymoon
to the attic filled my boyhood for a while.

One day I heard the plunk-plunk from our chestnut
tree, the gang all pocketing them for our pipes,
small fry on the block playing stickball, the flash
and thrust of limbs. I sat cross-legged before my
father's trunk and the wilderness of myself.
Signs I found in the tenacious silence of
things: I was the black-footed ferret, juggler,
harlequin: I was a touch on the padded
stairs, a balance of milkweed seed, Picasso
performance. With this strange fine figure of man
I had been playing follow the arrow and
capture the flag. Outside, someone was calling
ollie-ollie-oxen-free, and I was free
as a robin, a sun print on a swimmer,
the detached brownleaf and the unfallen snow.
Slyboots of that giant of my childhood, built
so long of limb and entangled in those dark
lidded privacies, I was equidistant
to 'love that makes the air light.' Chip of his strength.

Raymond Roseliep

FROM THE LIBRARY WINDOWS

I look down on the Iowa River.
It moves darkly past the empty
music building, waiting for the wail
of oboes,

eddies by the art gallery where
Elliot jades repose, inscrutable
and cool,

past the catacombic dorms
carved in cliffs.

It dumps dead branches,
empty Grainbelt cans. Sludge
collects against the willow branch
reaching for water.

Students cross bridges
in bright waves. They could grow up
in Steamboat Rock or Keokuk. Here
they are marked slightly,
ripples pass over.

Ann Struthers

OUT   OF   THIS   WORLD

astonishing
complexities:

a Volkswagen bus
full of greens

•

Iowa City crickets
September nights
don't have that much to say

but say it & say it & say it

"scribble scribble
eh   Mr Pound?"

•

Cheyenne,
Wyoming.

a known
town on Mars.

•

ah   Anna Bloom
sweet ginger muff

•

young girls walk
jointed
disjointed

no one to plug them in

don't let the exo-skeletals take them

they are the moon

•

"let's make it to the rock hole"
the spirit children sing
& men & women   in their bodies
do   that   thing

•

brother immortal
                    jellyfish
        "brighter than
                    the brightest star"

what do you know of wars
here on TV

poetry workshops   pills
the Naga question

or Dr Sigmund Freud
the famous hypnotist

there's none could cure you
of your ignorance

I mean that's great

we love you as you are

●

here
in the Upper Devonian Sea
life is quiet

even the thousands of hogs
make but little noise

●

dark blur girl
rushing
past in a car

a lifetime.
where was she going

●

hi—
late summer.
all
is forgiven.

●

Ovidius Naso
wrote a book

Sir Vincent Wigglesworth
created a giant caterpillar

here
I put them together

(you do too)

●

Thales of Miletus
loved
    this humid universe

there are
such advantages

    to walking on 2 legs

    & in carrying
        one's brain in one's head

let the galaxies
    ride!
      Thales

    it's been a long time
      between drinks

Anselm Hollo

A VISIT TO LLOYD IN AMANA

for Lloyd Quibble

1.   Amana's come to life again
    just after billboards. Corridas.
    Crossing of water, Aegean,
    Atlantic, Judy in my arms
    in various Barcelona
    rooms, Sam near drowning
    in the Court of the Lions
    of the great Alhambra

where girls of the harem
swam. (A German tourist
fished him out, sans red
boot, then asked me
for twenty bucks, I said
for my son
you can have it all,
take it all, this car,
this belt, these sun
glasses. *Nein, danke,*
nur zwanzig, danke.)
But that was in
another country.
Now we are land
locked, having crossed
waters, walked streets,
bedded down, whispered
in each other's ears,
conch shells—she is
Petworth-raised Turneresque
woman, a landscape aswirl
near water, a sunset returning.
Often we are children,
ghosts bring their names
to us, we are saying
vows naked as jaybirds
and getting in and out
of cars, and so
drive to Amana, westwards.

2.   We take one four nine North
at first, cross high yellow curbs
peculiar to Iowa, cause
of many fatal wrecks,
dentures and grey hair
flung through windshields,
severed locks of childhood too,
the birds gathering all

and making nests
out of both young and old.
We are successful, however,
in our turn, and ease on
to an upraised levee, a ribbon,
a bridge. We evade flood waters
to right and left, find,
as directed, company store,
winery, then Ox Yoke
Inn, where dangle loops
for two necks, two folks
who have decided
to love no others.
In the winery we sample
grape and rhubarb,
I like it dry, she likes
it sweet. She pokes a pin
in their giant map
for Petworth where she
lived, for Sussex
for petting near the sea
for Roman walls, for sex
and sweet wine and we've found
out where Lloyd is living
now.

3. The town's got corn crib wealth,
    tassels waving wild,
    sunshine mad on loving fuzz
    and silk,
    it cries out to the Mississippi
    to save it,
    take its picture
    for future generations,
    pack the picture in a trunk,
    pack the trunk in a steamboat,
    sink the steamboat
    in the Mississippi,

rely on others to find the boat,
find the corn, find the lost
sun, the day
we are seeking Lloyd's,
his house marked with the
                    PEACE
sign, we call upstairs
                    LLOYD

He leans down, says
                    Yeah, come on up.
We see stained glass
downstairs where others
live, their entrance is marked
                    EXIT

Place is nice, I say to Lloyd.
He says, fifty bucks, good deal.
He has a round oak
table, a flute
and music for Bach and God
Bless America.
He says: that's all
I can play but Laura's really
good and the landlord,
he's got six hundred gallons
of rhubarb wine in the basement,
let's drink it all.

4. Monday's slaughter day,
    Lloyd says, then their cries
    come through the walls.
    They know. Once calf
    got loose, knocked his head
    against the wall, ate the whole
    yard. I looked out,
    he called to me, *me*
    to save him. Then the butcher

came, Amana Colony's famous for
meat. He wouldn't listen.

Humane slaughter laws are for cars, I said,
looking out to where my Texas
headlights burned.
Skies there were still
friendly skies of, buttermilk
clouds.
Lloyd said: they put strychnine
in, that's why I feel
the death, my head's about to fall,
I wake up, jerk it up, or lie
down. Come back from where death
took me, Mr. Death. You have to trust
who gives you mescaline
or acid either.
Lloyd sits tailor-fashine,
needle in his claw,
has made elegant colored hippie coat
from mill scraps.
We discuss how rich
we could all get, going into
business, as if we
could go Main Street.
Lloyd says yeah and we
can get bottles on the city
dump and sell them too.
I know where the old
ones are, Civil War stuff,
both brown and blue.

5. Swigging rhubarb wine
    we find the Ox Yoke,
    waitress tells us we can't drink
    it 'because a neighbor
    sold it.' Lloyd tells us
    how to spot a narc, he's at

the next table, fat
and eating sauer kraut and braten.
We hear his skinny friend
(another narc, Lloyd whispers)
say: If you wanted to see
someone bust up
a meeting you should of seen
how Herb busted up
the meeting.

We pay cashier. What
have we got here? she asks,
an Indian? She's
Concerned
about Lloyd's headband.
I ask her how much cookbook
is, *Colony Recipes.*
She says two bucks.
I buy cookbook, my mother's
birthday.

We go out, onto old porch,
cider presses block
our way, plowshares
such as Grampa lifted, placed
behind his mules,
three ears of Indian
corn and a bull's dried
prick upon the wall.

6. We say farewell, leave Lloyd
to climb his stairs.
Once more we are shoving out,
we will inspect *Custer's Last Stand*
in Lone Tree bars
and hear what the barkeep
says about old Vietnam
and what is really done

to keep our cars in line.
Once more we are fed
from yellow curbs and onto
bridges like sausage.
We will not be the founders
of dynasties
I tell her, I break this news
to her gently.
Our thirty gallon crock
will never make a Ming.
She says she hopes Lloyd
and his group will prosper
in their commune. I say
Not in Ithaca, New York,
they won't.

7. All the small voices cry
in the wilderness
shuddering like the leaves
they are, concerned
as are small night animals
forgetting their own fates
to care for others, and the
waters ripple and say
too that they are voices
we have not stopped to hear

Iowa City, 1969
Kansas City, 1974

David Ray

FIRST SNOW

1

It is raining in the cornfields
the guinea are huddled in the sheds
wet leaves shining
in their eyes

Dogs bark along the fences
gourds rattle under dry hollyhocks
the whole world
has quivered into apple trees

In the barn
an old tramp is polishing his whistle
in the morning
he will wake to the cold of horses
breathing through their bridles
of terrible silver
and he will run through the snow
with his sack
to catch the bright little train
warming up in Milwaukee

2

I fall down in the tramp
of you begging
for bread and cheese
when the turkeys begin
their remarkable dance
in the moonlight
we'll be asleep in the yellow boxcar
bound for Oregon

3

I feel the little whistle
in your pocket
the snow is heavy on the trees
it is dark

a one legged moon
follows our tracks
it must feel like this
in the antarctic
when an old seal
is left alone for a million years

Ruth Doty

THE EIGHTY

(from We Have All Gone Away*)*

When human gleaning of the Eighty ended, the entire acreage became a grange for our field herd of black Angus. They'd find corn we hadn't, eat the rich slough grass, and munch the resprouting oats field before winter killed everything. We seldom fed more than fifty or sixty cattle, yet for the cattle drive to the Eighty all available children stood guard at each possible astray route along the way, waved hands and cried, "whoooosha! whoooosha!" hustling them along at a moderately excited pace. Out the farm road gate, filling up the thoroughfare, headed west. At the crossroads a quarter mile away, two boy sentinels stopped cars, spread arms wide to the loose animals. The older cattle knew where they were going and liked the idea, eager to be rid of our regular-hour bushel-basket feeding; glad to quit the familiar pastures clipped to the roots, tired of waiting for the tufts to hurry up and grow—knowing what loop in the fence allowed them to reach heads through for a morsel of forbidden, long ditch grass, or where a cowplop made the dark green blades delicious. After they'd all arrived safely, we shut the gate on their unfenced realm: eighty acres to move around on, the only shelter the leeward side of a strawstack created during July threshing and not very big; in a month they'd have demolished all of it. Here they were allowed to go primitive; after a time in the Eighty they were noticeably wilder-eyed, skittered when an automobile approached, or lumbered off like bison if a man came too near. They were on the range of their ancestors and reverting fast.

Winter was upon us when it was time to drive the herd home. The last freedoms of movement upon the soil were over for everybody, and we'd soon be struggling through drifts up to our ears. By late November the cattle looked fatter, their coats thickened to a rich, furry black, like the Alaska seal coats my two maiden aunts wore. The black, lowing herd, staccato hoofs on frozen ground, would surprisingly fill the farmyard from barns to garden fence. We were all cowboys then.

But one winter Uncle Jack left the herd in the Eighty too long. A terrible blizzard swept across the plains from the Rocky Mountains. We heard weather reports on the 6 A.M. news, and family counsel decided we shouldn't go to school, the roads would be closed. All of us were needed to rescue the cattle stranded in the Eighty. We bundled up in double overalls, one pulled over the other, buckle overshoes, blanket-lined jackets, and helmets with ear flaps, a muffler around mouth and nose. Only our eyes peeped out from below the leather helmet rim; if necessary, we could push up the wool cloth and still see through the interstices of weave. The women were alarmed for our safety, but the crisis of the herd in the Eighty was overriding. As we turned out the road gate in the Model A Ford, beyond the barrier of evergreens we could scarcely navigate the drifts. Great stream-lined banks, dunelike shapes, were alive and growing across the ditch, spuming snow. We gunned the motor to keep momentum, and when we reached the Eighty, found the murmuring cattle in a clump by the closed gate, reproachful over our late arrival. In their bones they'd felt the storm coming days before and wondered, no doubt, why *we* hadn't—life knowledge they possessed but which we'd deliberately moved away from in order to achieve a consciousness of ourselves, in order to use Nature for our purposes.

The cattle huddled with backs to the strong northwest wind, heads away from the sharp snow, which came streaking on a parallel with the ground. They were cattle-snowmen, every detail etched in frost, lashes hoary, whiskers and nostrils ice-encased; even with rumps to the storm, by morning they'd have suffocated from ice filling their noses. After we shoveled open the gate, they needed no encouragement; their leaders knew the direction of our warm barns and turned east without paying attention to me standing guard, not even a wrong lunge in fun.

Uncle Jack spotted the gangly, small calf, born perhaps two weeks previously, huddled close to its mother, the snow binding them together, encasing them in a womb of winter. Jack swooped the calf up in his arms, collapsing the stalky legs as you would a folding chair, and the frightened, half-dead baby sat there like those pictures in Sunday school books of the lamb in Jesus' arms. "Here, Ruthie, this one's for you," said Jack to my sister, who of course insisted on coming along with us boys on this adventure. She climbed into the back seat of the auto, the calf on her lap big as a dog, blue eyes blinking, and I marveled how the docile baby accepted any female love. The iced snow around his muzzle began to melt and he trembled all over. Ruth hugged him as she rubbed his coiled black hair. Though born here in the wilderness, he now knew domesticity was his true circumstance; he needed us in order to live. But I didn't carry it further: that his eventual death in the slaughterhouse in Sioux City was to be his inevitable fate, so that we could make our living.

Curtis Harnack

THE CATTLE GHOSTS

(Sioux City: I am standing where Armour's used to be)

where they came from once
they come from yet:
a place far off and quieter
for its few swallows
and peeled, face-sunken barns

in the spittled wombs of trucks
through Iowa's screaming nights
they come head on

to this louder land
of the kick and prod
and hammered breath

dying is a shy habit here
that goes on always:

the one with the face of a friend
the one with the mushroomed eye
the one with the limp

I am near them all
though the kill-floor heavens fall

David Allan Evans

THE OLD FAMILIES

We are members of the old families.
Our blood runs purple
Through four generations.
We preempted the land
On which your town now stands.

We built log cabins
Along the ravines
And drove ox teams to Fort Dodge
For supplies.
We sent for a parson and a teacher.

We fought the railroad when it came through
And we promoted our own real estate schemes.
The railroad built its own town—
And we built ours.

We had money to lend
And we organized banks.
The interest built our homes
And sent our daughters to Paris,
And our sons to Rome.
It paid for these stones.

We are members of the old families
And our bones lie in Riverview Cemetery.
Drop down honeysuckle, fern and wild sweet william.

Here is the first white child
Born in Algona.
Here is the stage coach driver.
The first mayor, the first parson,
And the first homesteaders.

We are the Calls, the Blackfords, the Inghams,
The Daltons, the Smiths,
The Hendersons, the Lessings, Heckerts, Hudsons,
McGetchies and the Kings.
Our blood runs purple through generations
And now . . .

There is a gray-haired old maid
And a few others, bearing new names—
A street loafer and a bankrupt;
The others have gone.

Count the stones, in a long row,
And read the gray names.
Kick your toe in the gravel path
And roll a stone
While you look north to the river and hills
In search of us.

There are two black lines
Up the north valley.
The stage coach went there.

We are members of the old families
And our bones lie
In Riverview Cemetery.

Raymond Kresensky

AT MY MOTHER'S GRAVE

Goldfinches lift from nowhere,
climb,
dip,
piping *per-chic-o-ree*
twice at the crest of each wave,
then are gone
from December sun,
leaving me lightfooted
light.

Before April bee
will roar thru my stringtied
violets,
spider bounce
on his homemade trampoline,
ballerina moth
figure my mother's grave,
or wind bring
the coupling *clank*
of I. C. coal cars
from the valley where
my mother's eyeblue
River eases by,
and things are things again:

I pocket the bone-rattle
of my beads,
catch mortal breath
within sight of my brother's
rococo roses,
candle parched and
incredible as waxen flesh,
and when my breath moves with
a wind moving a tiny
skull of autumn leaf
on checkerboard sod,
I give short shrift

to the boy in me
asking
how do I cope with a ghost.

Before night will touch the fallen
oak with its record of rings,
lower on my mother's grave,
reach me:
I will tend
light.

Filigree twig shadow
stirs like lace
on my hand and withered grass,
like lace in a tintype
for the eyes' appraisal,
sun splinters to
matchwood
in my gathering arms.
My mother relates to the
universe, this Iowa hill
and manchild:
flesh is shattered,
spirit refracted.

Fifty trillion
cells of me
rise with the Massbread
dough in my oven at home.
Goldfinches lift from nowhere,
climb,
dip,
lantern the abundant air.

Raymond Roseliep

PENSIONER: IOWA

O the tracks run east to Illinois
and west to Nebraska; all the boys
have taken all the girls away,
and the mail comes every other day.

When I was born my mother died;
they had to open up her side
to get me out; she never healed.
Her grave is under a soybean field.

My father was a pioneer,
and I was born and raised right here.
When I was ten I found him dead;
our cow had kicked him in the head.

When I was twelve I took his gun
and shot a stone-drunk Indian.
He'd swiped a crock of salted meat,
and I left him for the hogs to eat.

I drank away my father's farm
and my mother's grave; I meant no harm.
I get a check from the government
that buys me beer and pays the rent.

O the tracks run east to Illinois
and west to Nebraska; all the boys
are rolling with their wives in bed
and all the pioneers are dead.

Ted Kooser

LANDLORD'S DEATH

He bought a Victorian mansion on Grand,
    unplanned, and had it
        compartmentalized.

In Des Moines, he is not remembered
    except in a will & lawyer's bill
        where his bequest of Everything to wife
           is authorized.

One spring night he got in his '49 Cadillac
    out back; his wife found him in a state
        of somnambulance & called an ambulance;
           nevertheless, he was forever already
                immobilized.

Tenants continued to take in mail &
    watched his chihuahua ail, while
        the spring sky bolted over Iowa;
        his widow left, to drive West,
      before he could be
        sentimentalized.

Izora Corpman

THE FARMER'S WIDOW: A LAMENT

    Why leapt ye, ye high hills, upon the morn
My beloved himself was born,
And grew as the lily casting forth its root,
And covered the face of the world with fruit?
    I remember his most gradual gesture,
    The precision of his limbs:
How he'd romp through a shower of apricots,
Dance wild through the leaves.

Then he would plant pleasant plants, and keep the sheep;
And in the evening would he set forth wheat,
When to me he'd fly as the eagle that hastens to eat,
And sing my praises upon the timbrel and the harp.

Oh he, the peccant angel, with a pleasing sorcery, could charm:
Now he's dead and gone.

And the earth mourns and fades away,
And the world languishes and fades away:
The heavens grow dark, and the mountains tremble,
And all the birds have fled. Only the screech owl rests here.
Far away, the sparrow has found a house,
And the swallow a nest for herself, where she may lay her young.
And I? A pelican of the wilderness, an owl of the desert:
My heart is melted in the midst of my bowels.

—He blew a reed into my bowels.
I linked steps to his steps,
And our valley were covered with corn—

Why leapt ye, ye high hills, upon the morn
My beloved himself was born,
And grew as the lily casting forth its root,
And covered the face of the world with fruit?

Carol Hebald

OPAL EGLI RENNIE
1919–1971

Dead of arthritis and cortisone
too young. Now I remember the Christmas
turkey she carved up for the clan, how
around the kitchen table she, Mom, Eleanor
and I giggled that we all preferred, over
all the other pieces, the fowl's plump
back-end, the rich juice of tail. "My land,"

Opal laughed as we drew straws. "Is that
hereditary?" I wanted to know; she suspected
so. Oh the pumpkin pies she dished out!
Statistics claim my aunt didn't have
children. The way Mom tells it, Opal
had nine: the brothers and two sisters
she was eldest of; how they'd run to her
with hurt fingers or feelings, a special

blossom or dream. After she married,
they'd visit her—sometimes whole weekends.
She'd greet company in apron and smiles
open as her own back door. At home
in Pocahontas, Iowa, she saved postcards
from all over.

       I think of that last August,
glad I and my boy spent a day of it
with her; how she thanked us for coming,
her round friendly body at the door, waving
us back to Colorado, her eyes adrift in the sun,

doe-brown, brown as any German Egli's ever were.

Victoria McCabe

FARMER, RETIRED

A man under the town clock
on Main Street loiters
before a bucket of lilies
gracing the drugstore entry,
never told they are plastic.

He can smell them: heady as plowed earth
or fluted lettuce a housewife tended

or even pears plunking outside the bedroom.
He is a tintype, still unfooled
so long as bees keep their appointment in his blood.

Raymond Roseliep

TO THE CHILDREN AT THE FAMILY ALBUM

Across Grandmother Ingersoll's face
the Civil War happened. Events crisscrossed
her mouth; and the names of battles would
stir in her eyes, herself part slave, part
free (like me, children, like you—our mouth
hers but our mind running freedom road).

Those days back home they got the moon's
report across Iowa: deportment
of corn shocks—feathers or corn leaf?—
and oak with its fingers out in vain
to hold nothing, then sigh. All that
frozen country went under, winter
only a sound, the pond a kettledrum.

Children, events can find any face,
and many as leaves are, a little weight
at last will make them fall. A hand
that reaches with love can hurt
any dear face in the world,
as love raked across the Civil War
and into the face of Grandmother Ingersoll.

William Stafford

ELEGY

Listen, my friend, shuttered in
your small room, winter is gone.
I tell you spring now wakens
furred buds on the boughs of pussy
willows, at the edge of the field a lark
nests among weed stalks harsh with
the wind's whistle. Maples unfold
new leaves, oaks wait for the warm
May sun, violets rise from curled
clusters and wild plums cover thorns
with white blossoms, even watercress
shows color at the spring's mouth.
You have seen flocks of geese print
their flight on the wide innocent sky
over Iowa, and bundled farmers on bright
red tractors smooth fields for sowing.
Listen, you can hear the cock pheasant's
cry while April rain sends up shooting
stars and jack-in-the-pulpits. Fill your
mind's eye with the hill beyond the big
barn where she last watched an autumn sunset.

James Hearst

WORSHIPPERS OF WHEAT

(from A Son of the Middle Border*)*

As I look back over my life on that Iowa farm the song of the
reaper fills a large place in my mind. We were all worshippers of
wheat in those days. The men thought and talked of little else between seeding and harvest, and you will not wonder at this if you
have known and bowed down before such abundance as we then
enjoyed.

Deep as the breast of a man, wide as the sea, heavy-headed,

supple-stocked, many-voiced, full of multitudinous, secret, whispered colloquies,—a meeting place of winds and of sunlight,—our fields ran to the world's end.

We trembled when the storm lay hard upon the wheat, we exulted as the lilac shadows of noon-day drifted over it! We went out into it at noon when all was still—so still we could hear the pulse of the transforming sap as it crept from cool root to swaying plume. We stood before it at evening when the setting sun flooded it with crimson, the bearded heads lazily swirling under the wings of the wind, the mousing hawk dipping into its green deeps like the eagle into the sea, and our hearts expanded with the beauty and the mystery of it,— and back of all this was the knowledge that its abundance meant a new carriage, an addition to the house or a new suit of clothes.

Hamlin Garland

LOSING WSUI

Driving East, and I begin
to lose the string quartet put out
by University Radio, WSUI;

those grave clear notes, making
a Lithuania of these black
Mid-Western fields must now

compete with blurred
upswellings of sound, tumorous
commercial heavings, as saws

sobbing into the trunks
of trees, women swaying
packed with tobacco, creaming

all the sparkling parks
their world offers. The beams
the tall transmitter spits

so strongly out near home
begin to falter now, cowards
of distance, and the rich

stream of kilowatts withers
visibly almost, a flickering
of birds turning for home

through the November air.
And now the voice of your
announcer, Larry Barrett, displaying

no panic, begins to be
sucked under by a quicksand
of muck, money music, noise

fronds at his throat, a whole
ruptured jungle of sound
springing up around the bright

tin huts our minds rent. I
will not be driven to the edge
of Iowa by the urgent

melancholy of cellos after
all. Larry is sinking
fast now, still stately, swallowed

like a pagoda. A last
gargle of vowels, and the inane
other America takes over, goodbye

WSUI, farewell Larry, remember
me to Albinoni.

Michael Dennis Browne

SUNSET

The cows
sink into the meadow,
small violet ships.
Pigs and their sticky night sounds
lie down together in their wallow.
The old dog,
smelling like all animals,
follows silence from barn to barn.

Through the stillness
swallows carry the last light down
on thin wings of fire.
The red night.
The blue night.

A gray little whirlwind
stirs in the oat field.
Corn tassels tremble.
The cool north wind
sets me adrift.

Sounds of earth move me,
dreaming shadows of meadowlarks
move me. The air is alive
with the breath of animals.

Jim Heynen

A DO-IT-YOURSELF POEM

In Colorado once, Iowans,
farm-hungry, scooped up that western dirt
in their calloused hands. It was crumbling and richly black.
They staked claim, out-waited the winter,
waited out the summer, and almost starved.

They had the seed; they had the plows and the prayers
and the babies coming, yes, and the strong arms
and the willing backs. What were they waiting for?
Rain. That was all. And it never came,
and never would. Now you go on, like they did:

say, "That's life."
Make your own metaphor.

Nancy Price

CONTRIBUTORS

JOE DAVID BELLAMY lives in Canton, New York, where he teaches at St. Lawrence University and edits *Fiction International*. He has been published in the *Paris Review, Prairie Schooner*, and the *Iowa Review*, and is the author of *The New Fiction*.

RICHARD BISSELL holds mate's and pilot's licenses, all tonnage, for the Mississippi and Monongahela rivers, and once operated a towing and transport company with a tug named "Coal Queen." He was born in Dubuque, Iowa, and was graduated from Phillips Exeter Academy and Harvard. Bissell's several books include *7½ Cents* (which later became the Broadway play and movie "Pajama Game") and *My Life on the Mississippi; or, Why I am Not Mark Twain*. He now lives in Boothbay Harbor, Maine.

JOSEPHINE EDITH BROWN (1878–1964) was born on a farm near Shelby, Iowa. She attended rural one-room schools and was herself a teacher at the age of 18. Later, in 1899, she enrolled at Iowa State College (Iowa State University), majoring in home economics. She married Richard Hopkins in 1906 and moved with him to Troy, New York, where she lived until her death.

MICHAEL DENNIS BROWNE was born in England and attended Hull and Oxford before he came to the United States in 1967 for the M.A. degree at the University of Iowa. His poems have been published in *The Atlantic, American Review*, and *Antaeus*. *The Wife of Winter* is his first book of poetry.

RAYMOND CARVER's poetry has been collected into two books—*Near Klamath* and *Winter Insomnia*—but he thinks of himself primarily as a writer of fiction. His stories have appeared in *Esquire, December, Harper's Bazaar,* the *O'Henry Prize Stories of 1973 and 1974, Best Little Magazine Fiction 1970 and 1971,* and elsewhere. He was born in Clatskanie, Oregon. He has been both student and visiting lecturer at the University of Iowa.

G. S. SHARAT CHANDRA was born in India and now makes his home in the United States. He is Poet-in-Residence, Washington State University, Pullman. *The Wolf's Sniff* and *Once or Twice,* chapbooks of his poetry, are forthcoming.

JOSEPHINE CLARE was born in Germany and was graduated from high school there. With her husband, Anselm Hollo, she has translated William Carlos Williams' *Paterson* into German. Her own poems have been collected in *deutschland* and *deutschland & other places.*

IZORA CORPMAN lived for a year in an old Victorian mansion in Des Moines, where she kept a yellow bird named Bartholomew and taught at Drake. She now lives in Oak Park, Michigan. Her poems have appeared in *New: American & Canadian Poetry.* She was born in Detroit and attended the University of Michigan.

R. R. CUSCADEN was born in Chicago and has always lived in Illinois. He is architecture critic for the *Chicago Sun-Times.* From 1960 to 1966 he published and edited *Midwest.* His poems have appeared in *The North American, Minnesota,* and *Chicago* reviews, among others, and in the chapbooks *Poem for a Ten Pound Sailfish* and *Ups & Downs of a Third Baseman.*

ANN DARR was born in Bagley, Iowa. She was graduated from the University of Iowa. Her poems have been collected in *St Ann's Gut* and *The Myth of a Woman's Fist.* She now lives with her family in Chevy Chase, Maryland.

STEPHEN DOBYNS was born in East Orange, New Jersey. He attended Shimer College, Wayne State University, and obtained the M.F.A. degree from the University of Iowa. His first book of poetry, *Concurring Beasts,* won the Lamont Award for 1971. He is author also of a novel, *A Man of Little Evils.*

MARK DOTY was born in Maryville, Tennessee, and grew up in various rural towns in southern Tennessee. His poems have appeared in *kayak, The Wisconsin Review,* and elsewhere. He and his wife Ruth live in Des Moines where he works as a teacher for a day care service.

RUTH DOTY was born in Louisiana. A graduate of the University of Houston, her work has appeared in *Anglo-Welsh Review, New Orleans Review,* and *Apple,* among others. She now teaches at Drake University.

PAUL ENGLE has written ten books of poetry in addition to books of reminiscence, children's stories, and an opera libretto. He was born in Cedar Rapids, the son of parents who came from farming families. His first book, *Worn Earth,* was the Yale Series of Younger Poets selection in 1932. His most recent collection is *A Woman Unashamed.* Engle was educated at Coe College, the University of Iowa, and Columbia. He was a Rhodes Scholar at Oxford in 1933–1936. He is now director of the International Writing Program at the University of Iowa. (Some of the lines from "For the Iowa Dead" have been put on bronze plates and installed in Iowa City at the Memorial Union together with the names of the war dead of the University of Iowa.)

DAVE ETTER attended the University of Iowa. He was born in California and now resides in Geneva, Illinois. Of his work he has said, "I am obsessed with the American Middle West and most of my poems are the result of that obsession." He has published five collections of poetry, the latest being *Crabtree's Woman*.

DAVID ALLAN EVANS was born in Sioux City, Iowa, and holds degrees from Morningside College and the University of Iowa. His poems have appeared in *Esquire, The North American Review, Poetry Northwest,* and elsewhere. He lives in Brookings, South Dakota, and teaches at South Dakota State University.

DONALD FINKEL says that "'Target Practice' was written partially in response to a whimsical assertion of Paul Engle's that it is metrically gauche to make the name of Iowa the last word in a line of verse." The author of seven books of poetry (the latest is *A Mote in Heaven's Eye*), Finkel is Poet-in-Residence at Washington University, St. Louis. He was born in New York City but, he says, he has been drawn inexplicably, since the tender age of seventeen, to the cities of the plain (Chicago, Iowa City, Urbana, St. Louis), in the last of which he now resides with his wife, the poet and novelist Constance Urdang.

HAMLIN GARLAND (1860–1940) was born in Wisconsin and reared on a succession of pioneer farms in Iowa and South Dakota. He attended Cedar Valley Seminary in Osage from 1876 to 1881. The thirty stories in *Main-Travelled Roads* (1891), *Prairie Folks* (1893), and *Wayside Courtships* (1897), plus the four volumes in his "Middle Border" series, constitute most of his best work. He received the Pulitzer Prize for *A Daughter of the Middle Border* in 1922, and on July 3, 1931, a marker in his honor was placed on the old Cedar Valley Seminary grounds.

GARY GILDNER came to Iowa in 1966, the year he began to write poetry. His stories have appeared in *December, New Letters, Chicago Review, Best Little Magazine Fiction 1970;* his poems have been collected in *First Practice, Digging for Indians,* and *Nails.* He was born in Michigan and attended Michigan State. He teaches at Drake.

DANIEL HALPERN lives in New York City, where he edits *Antaeus.* His first book of poetry is called *Traveling on Credit.*

CURTIS HARNACK was born near LeMars, Iowa, in 1927—in a farmhouse handbuilt by his prairie sodbreaker grandfather. He attended Grinnell College and Columbia, and served in the Navy late in World War II (out of Port Chicago). "The Eighty," printed here, is part of a chapter from his most recent work, *We Have All Gone Away,* which tells about his early years in Iowa. He also has written two novels set in the Midwest—*The Work of an Ancient Hand* and *Love and Be Silent*—plus a book about Iran, *Persian Lions, Persian Lambs.* He is executive director of Yaddo. He lives in Saratoga Springs, New York, and in New York City with his wife, writer Hortense Calisher.

JAMES HEARST was born at Maplehearst Farm near Cedar Falls. He was graduated from Iowa State Teachers College (University of Northern Iowa), where he now teaches. Five books of his poetry have been published; among them: *Country Men, Man and His Field,* and *A Single Focus.*

CAROL HEBALD was a successful actress before becoming an English major at City College in New York. She has written two novellas—*Asylum* and *Clara Kleinschmidt* (excerpts from the former and all of the latter appearing in *The North American Review)*—and is currently at work on a full-length novel, *The Good Neighbor.* She lived for a time in Cedar Falls, where she taught at the University of Northern Iowa. Her poems have appeared in the *Antioch* and *Massachusetts* reviews.

PHILLIP HEY teaches writing in Sioux City, Iowa. He was born in Dixon, Illinois, and holds the M.F.A. degree from the University of Iowa. *Field* and *Hearse,* among others, have published his poems.

JIM HEYNEN grew up on a farm near Sioux Center, Iowa. His poems have appeared in *Prairie Schooner, Sunday Clothes,* and *Kansas Quarterly,* among others. He has taught in Idaho, Michigan, and Alaska, and now lives with his wife Carol, in Oregon.

ANSELM HOLLO, born in Finland, has lived in Sweden, Germany, Austria, Spain, Britain, and, since 1967, in the United States, where he has taught at State University of New York, Buffalo; Bowling Green State; and the University of Iowa. In addition to his own poetry, he has translated from German, French, Spanish, Swedish, and Finnish. His books include *Sensation 27, Maya,* and *Any Day Now.* He now lives in Geneva, New York, with his wife, the poet Josephine Clare.

MARK JOHNSON holds a degree in art from Buena Vista College. He was born in Alta, Iowa. *Sunday Clothes, Corduroy,* and *Poetry NOW* have published his poems.

JOHN JUDSON's "Morgan's Canes" was written in Iowa, he says, and is "about a composite Maine memory/fiction and the farmer on whose tenant farm we lived for three years in Solon. Later I incorporated it in a play, *West of Burnam, South of Troy,* which again was rewritten into a radio play which won a National Public Radio EARPLAY award last year." Judson is editor and founder of NORTHEAST/Juniper Books and teaches at the University of Wisconsin, LaCrosse.

DONALD JUSTICE was born in Miami, Florida, and grew up there. His first book, *The Summer Anniversaries,* received the Lamont Award for 1959. He is author also of *Night Light* and *Departures,* and edited *The Collected Poems of Weldon Kees.* He teaches in the Writers Workshop of the University of Iowa.

BERNARD KAPLAN is the author of *Prisoners of This World,* a book of short stories. *Obituaries,* a collection of short fiction, is forthcoming. He was born in the Bronx, grew up in New Jersey, and lived in Iowa for three years. He says, "I lost my eastern provinciality in Iowa. It was an important moment in a hospitable state. My roots will inevitably lie in the cluttered northeast, but I consider Iowa my second, open home."

GEORGE KEITHLEY, born in Chicago, is the author of two books of poetry, *The Donner Party* and *Song in a Strange Land,* and the stage adaptation of *The Donner Party.* He now lives with his wife in Chico, California, where he teaches at California State.

DAVE KELLY was born in Michigan and attended Michigan State and the University of Iowa. His poems have been collected in *Instructions for Viewing a Solar Eclipse* and in a number of chapbooks. He now lives in Geneseo, New York, with his wife, Sylvia.

x. j. KENNEDY "is not a native of Iowa," he says, "but a longtime visitor and observer of the place." He was born in Dover, New Jersey. He has edited *An Introduction to Poetry* and, with his wife, Dorothy, the magazine *Counter/Measures. Nude Descending a Staircase,* his first book, won the 1961 Lamont Award. He teaches at Tufts.

BERTHA KIRKENDALL was born in Albion, Iowa, where she has lived all her life. Her sister Lida remembers that Bertha was the best rope-skipper in the whole town, and that when she came home from school at night she brought in corncobs and kindling for the supper fire, without being reminded by their mother. "Now that Bertha is older," says Lida, "there are petunias along her walk, rows of canned goods on her cellar shelves, and she can come up with a tea party for grand-nieces and -nephews at the turn of a doorknob. Stop by. The cookie jar is always full."

PETER KLAPPERT's first book, *Lugging Vegetables to Nantucket,* was the Yale Series of Younger Poets selection in 1970. His poems have appeared in *Armadillo, The New Yorker, The Trojan Horse,* and elsewhere. He holds two graduate degrees from the University of Iowa.

JOHN KNOEPFLE is the author of *Rivers into Islands, The Intricate Land,* and *Whetstone.* He was born in Cincinnati. His children's books include *Dogs & Cats & Things Like That* and *Our Street Feels Good.* He teaches at Sangamon State University in Illinois.

TED KOOSER edits *The New Salt Creek Reader* and works full time as an underwriter for an insurance company. He was born in Ames, Iowa, and attended Iowa State University. His poems have been collected in *Official Entry Blank, Twenty Poems,* and *A Local Habitation and a Name.* He lives in Lincoln, Nebraska.

LAWRENCE KRAMER says "I was born in 1939 in Newton, Iowa, where my father managed a dime store and my grandfather was a blacksmith. My family has lived in Iowa since the middle of the nineteenth century. There is an extremely small town, Ells, tucked away in a forgotten corner of Crawford County that is named for my great grandfather. To me that has always been important." Kramer is currently teaching in San Bernardino, California.

RAYMOND KRESENSKY (1897–1955) was born and grew up in Algona, Iowa. He earned degrees from Coe College and McCormack Seminary in Chicago, and during the Depression edited *Iowa: A Guide to the Hawkeye State,* under the WPA Writers project. The year after his death, *Selected Poems* (with an introductory essay by E. L. Mayo) appeared.

ERNEST KROLL is a former newspaperman and U.S. Government official, now retired. He has published three books of poetry—*Cape Horn and Other Poems, The Pauses of the Eye,* and *Fifty Fraxioms.* He lives in Washington, D.C.

JOSEPH LANGLAND grew up in Highland Township in Winneshiek County, Iowa, on a farm that provided the setting for "The Wheel of Summer." His first book of poetry, *The Green Town,* was nominated for the National Book Award; his second, *The Wheel of Summer,* received the

Melville Cane Award. His work has appeared in a great number of publications, among them *The Atlantic* and *Virginia Quarterly Review*. He was born in Spring Grove, Minnesota, and now teaches at the University of Massachusetts.

JOHN LOGAN was born in Red Oak, Iowa. He has written stories, a book for children, and five volumes of poetry, the most recent of which is *The Anonymous Lover*. He teaches at the State University of New York, Buffalo, and edits *Choice*.

VICTORIA MC CABE's poems in this anthology are from a new book she is writing called *The Dirt Book*. She believes, with Theodore Roethke, that "we need more barnyard poets." She was born in Fort Dodge, Iowa, and grew up around Clare. Her first book was *Victorian Poems*. She now lives with her husband in Tucson, Arizona.

E. L. MAYO was born in Boston; he was graduated *magna cum laude* from the University of Minnesota. A distinguished poet, teacher, critic, and friend to poets, Mayo's work has appeared in dozens of publications over the past forty years, and in four books: *The Diver, The Center is Everywhere, Summer Unbound*, and *Selected Poems*. Since 1947 Mayo has lived with his wife Myra in Des Moines, where, until his retirement in 1974, he taught at Drake.

MYRA MAYO was born in Aberdeen, Scotland; after 1914 she lived mostly in St. Paul, Minnesota. She attended Macalester College and the University of Minnesota, earning the B.A. and M.A. degrees. Her poems have appeared in *Motive* and *North American Mentor*.

ROBERT MEZEY lives in the Wasatch Mountains in Utah with his wife and family. He was educated at Kenyon College and at the University of Iowa. His books of poetry are *The Lovemaker* (winner of the Lamont Award in 1960), *White Blossoms, Favors, A Book of Dying*, and *The Door Standing Open*. He is also an editor of the anthologies *Naked Poetry* and *New Naked Poetry*. He was born in Philadelphia.

JACK MUSGROVE, director of the Iowa Historical Department, Historical Museum and Archives Division, was born in Iowa City and educated at the University of Iowa. He and his wife, Mary, have collaborated on several articles dealing with wildlife, anthropology, and Indian history, and on a book, *Waterfowl of Iowa,* published by the Iowa State Conservation Commission. Mary also attended the University of Iowa. She is on the staff of the *Des Moines Register and Tribune*.

NANCY PRICE is not a native Iowan but has lived here often in her life, and continuously since 1955. She was on the faculty of the University of Northern Iowa from 1964 to 1968, then left teaching to write her first novel, *A Natural Death*. Her poems have appeared in such magazines as *The Nation, Saturday Review,* and *The Atlantic*.

DAVID RAY was born in Sapulpa, Oklahoma. He has taught at several schools and traveled widely, and now lives in Kansas City, where he edits *New Letters. From the Hungarian Revolution, A Poetry Reading Against the Vietnam War*, and *Richard Wright: Impressions and Perspectives* are among the anthologies he has edited or coedited. His own poems have been collected in *X-Rays, Dragging the Main*, and *Gathering Firewood*. He was educated at the University of Chicago.